Test Your Child's Abilities

Test Your Child's Abilities

IQ Tests for Children Aged 10–15

Hans Eysenck and Darrin Evans

Colour Library

Thorsons
An Imprint of HarperCollins*Publishers*
77-85 Fulham Palace Road,
Hammersmith, London W6 8JB

1160 Battery Street,
San Francisco, California 94111-1213

Published by Thorsons 1996

CLD 20068

This edition published in 1996 for
Colour Library Direct,
Godalming Business Centre,
Woolsack Way,
Godalming,
Surrey GU7 1XW.

A catalogue record for this book is available from the
British Library

ISBN 1-85833-573-6

Printed in Great Britain by Woolnough Bookbinding Ltd,
Irthlingborough.

Contents

Acknowledgements

The authors wish to acknowledge the help given by the staff and students of Dulwich College and Sevenoaks School in the standardization of the tests.

Introduction

Intelligence and the IQ

Your child's intelligence is one of his or her most precious possessions, although other qualities, such as honesty, decency and a capacity to love and be loved, may be equally important. Intelligence alone is certainly not enough: Lenin, Mao Tsetung, Hitler, Mussolini and many other dictators were far from unintelligent, and there have been many intelligent criminals, such as those who have illegally made millions on the stock exchange.

Nor is high intelligence a guarantee of achievement. Also required are persistence, hard work, the ability to get on with others and perhaps a certain amount of creativity. Intelligence is important but not *all* important. Intelligence alone will not make your child happy.

Why Is Intelligence Important?

Intelligence largely determines how well you will do at school and, if you get that far, at university. It is a fundamental ingredient in doing well in your training for any profession. The intelligent may not always be successful, but the successful are usually intelligent. For more on the importance of intelligence, *see page 4*.

Can we define intelligence? Critics sometimes say that psychologists cannot agree on the meaning of 'intelligence', but this is untrue. In a recent survey of over 600 experts who were asked to list important elements of intelligence, over 99 per cent listed abstract thinking or reasoning; 98 per cent listed problem-solving ability; 90 per cent listed capacity to acquire knowledge. These qualities are precisely what common sense regards as the essence of 'intelligence' – and has done since Cicero used the term *intelligentia* 2,000 years ago. What psychologists have tried to do has been to refine the definition and to *measure* intelligence; they have not changed the meaning of the term.

Intellectual ability varies between individuals. Even schoolchildren know that some of their fellows are bright, others average and some dull*. Adults, too, have little trouble in recognizing which of their friends and acquaintances are more intelligent than others. Differences in children's intelligence, ranging from very bright to very dull, present great social and educational problems. Should children

*The use of the term 'dull' is intended scientifically rather than emotively.

be taught in 'mixed-ability' classes with children of all levels of competence, or should we use some method of selection to bring together children of roughly the same degree of ability? Is the concept of the 'comprehensive' school meaningful and realistic, or should we opt for the tripartite system of schooling which segregates pupils according to ability into grammar, secondary modern and 'technical' schools? Debates are usually based on political convictions, but factual considerations should perhaps be allowed to play a more important part than they have done in the past.

The Nature of Intelligence

Right from the beginning of attempts to measure intelligence there has been an absolutely fundamental controversy. Conveniently, it can be identified with the two protagonists who established the contrasting theories which have governed the field since the beginning of the 20th century. Protagonist one is Sir Francis Galton, cousin of Charles Darwin and universal genius. For him, intelligence was a unitary mental ability underlying all cognitive (mental) work, largely inherited from one's parents and measurable by biological tests, such as reaction times.

Protagonist two was Alfred Binet, a French psychologist who worked for the Ministry of Education investigating the link between mental retardation and poor scholastic performance. He viewed intelligence as the sum of several different abilities or functions, such as judgment, memory and perception. He also included qualities which we would hardly link to intelligence nowadays, such as suggestibility. 'Intelligence' appeared as a rather artificial average of all these and other 'faculties'. Binet believed that teaching and experience played an important part in the acquisition of these faculties; he did not really consider heredity in his work, although he did not deny its possible role. His most important contribution was his method of measuring intelligence, which was far more successful than Galton's, and is still the standard method used in all mental tests.

Mental Age and Chronological Age

Binet's difficulty in measuring these faculties separately led him in another, quite different, direction. He noted that, as children get older, they are more able to solve problems, reason abstractly and learn quickly; in other words, they become brighter on some absolute scale. This led him to define a child's 'mental age' (MA) – the intellectual level at which a child functions. A bright six-year-old might be functioning at the level of an average eight-year-old; this would give him or her the mental age of eight, although his or her 'chronological age' (CA) would be only six.

The difference indicated his or her mental superiority. Later on, William Stern introduced the concept of the 'intelligence quotient' (IQ), which is defined as a ratio of mental and chronological age, multiplied by 100 to get rid of the decimal point:

$$MA \div CA \times 100$$

How can we measure MA? This is where Binet made his most important contribution. He devised miniature problems that could be solved in a relatively short time, did not require specific scholastic knowledge and would be of interest to the children tested. Thus for five-year-olds, the problem might be to find a lost ball in a circular park represented on the page by a circle with an opening to indicate the gate. Any systematic search indicated by pencil marks in the circle (ever-decreasing circles; up-and-down movement covering all of the ground) was counted as a 'correct' answer; vague, uncoordinated marks were considered 'incorrect'. Hundreds of such problems were given to children and the 'age value' of each was determined. This was done by seeing at what age the problem is solved by the average child. In other words, if at age five, 50 per cent of children solve the 'lost ball' problem, it has an age value of five years. By determining the 'age value' of the problems correctly solved by a given child, we can determine his or her MA, and hence his or her IQ.

What Does the Child's IQ Mean?

By definition, the average child must have an IQ of 100 because MA = CA for the average child. If you had a child of eight with an MA of 10, the IQ would be 125. A child of 12 with an MA of 10 would have an IQ of 83. Figure 1 shows the distribution of the IQ in the population and the proportion of children in each part.

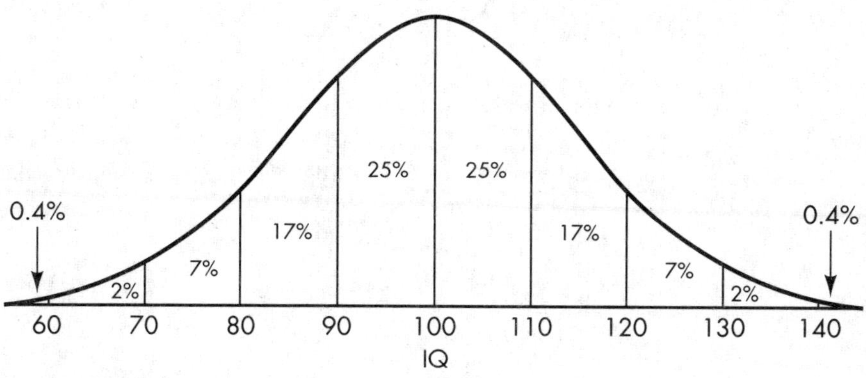

Figure 1. The distribution of IQ in the population (percentages rounded up).

Twenty-five per cent of all children have IQs between 90 and 100, and another 25 per cent between 100 and 110; thus 50 per cent are roughly 'average' in their intelligence. Those above 110 are relatively bright; those below 90, relatively dull. Four people in a thousand have an IQ of above 140 and are highly gifted. Figure 1 also shows another 0.4 per cent as having an IQ below 60. This is not quite accurate, as very low IQs arising from birth accidents, foetal poisoning and other disasters that may injure the growing cortex of the foetus or the newly-born have been added to it, creating a secondary group to those who are naturally very dull.

	Mean	SD	
Accountant	128	11.7	
Lawyer	128	10.9	
Auditor	125	11.2	
Reporter	124	11.7	Middle-class Occupations
Chief clerk	124	11.7	
Teacher	122	12.8	
Draughtsman	122	12.8	
Pharmacist	120	15.2	
Book-keeper	120	13.1	
Toolmaker	112	12.5	
Machinist	110	16.1	
Foreman	110	16.7	
Aeroplane mechanic	109	14.9	
Electrician	109	15.2	Skilled working-class occupations
Lathe operator	108	15.5	
Sheet metal worker	108	15.3	
Mechanic	106	16.0	
Riveter	104	15.1	
Painter, general	98	18.7	
Cook & baker	97	20.8	
Truckdriver	96	19.7	
Labourer	96	20.1	Semi-skilled working-class occupations
Barber	95	20.5	
Lumberjack	95	19.8	
Farmhand	91	20.7	
Miner	91	20.1	
Teamster	88	19.6	

Table 1. Mean IQs of members of different occupations. SD (standard deviation) indicates the range of IQs around the mean.

What does the IQ mean socially and professionally? Children would need an IQ of around 115 or above to succeed at university or medical school, or to qualify as a lawyer. Top runners would need something around 130 or above. Other factors are also very important, such as putting in enough hard work to fulfil potential. A person with an IQ of 115 who works very hard may out-perform an inherently lazy high-flyer with an IQ of 135. A poor person with a high IQ may have to work his or her way through college and simply not have enough time to study adequately. IQ is never the *only* factor determining success, although it may be the single most important factor.

Table 1 shows the average IQs of people working in various occupations. These range from accountant and lawyer to miner and teamster. The IQs follow roughly the classification of middle-class (white-collar) occupations through skilled working-class to semi-skilled working-class (blue-collar) occupations. Although they are not very surprising, there is one interesting feature. Under the heading 'SD', which stands for standard deviation, are given the range of IQs around the mean for all occupations; the smaller the SD, the smaller the observed deviations from the mean for that group. Note how SD increases as IQ decreases. In other words, there are few dull accountants or lawyers (because of all the exams they have to pass!), but there are many bright or very bright miners, farmhands or barbers. For various reasons, such people are in occupations below their ability level. They may have missed out on education; they may have been lazy, suffered prolonged illness or just been unlucky. Occupation is an uncertain indicator of IQ.

How Accurate Is IQ Measurement?

When properly carried out by experts using the appropriate tests, IQ measurement is remarkably accurate – to within three to five points of the true figure. For practical purposes this is quite close enough. Consider measuring your height. This may give different results depending on the time of day you carry out your measurement as the spine becomes compressed during the day, making a difference of 1–2 centimetres. There is proportionately a greater degree of (unavoidable) inaccuracy in measuring your height than in calculating the IQ. Even though the results of IQ testing can be affected by changes in degree of alertness and arousal related to the time of day, the differences are slight. If you measure your child's IQ now and then again a year or two later, the difference in the score should be no more than five points.

Critics sometimes suggest that the IQ measures nothing but the ability to do IQ tests. This is clearly not the case. As we have seen, there is a close relation between IQ and occupation *(see Table 1)*, and many studies have demonstrated the strong link between IQ and scholastic achievement. It is sometimes suggested that IQ simply reflects school learning, and that the IQ must therefore mirror scholastic achievement, but this too is untrue. Consider the Isle of Wight experiment in which IQ tests were given to all children at the age of five, i.e. *before* they went to school. The children were tested again at the age of 16, and their achievements were noted throughout their schooling. It was found that the IQ of the five-year-olds predicted with considerable precision the child's scholastic achievement, as well as his or her IQ at 16. It is IQ that produces scholastic achievement, not the other way around.

Nature and Nurture of Intelligence

The stress laid by Galton on heredity (nature) and by Binet on environment (nurture) in the genesis of intellectual differences has led to an absurd battle of nature versus nurture. Both must be involved at all times in the determination of differences in intelligence, so the only permissible questions are: which is the more important, at any given time and for any given population?; and how are the effects of either nature or nurture produced in specific detail? A third permissible question relates to the interaction of nature and nurture. If little Johnny goes to the library and takes out lots of science books because he wants to become a scientist, or if little Mary persuades her parents to let her take music lessons because she wants to become a pianist, can we regard these as environmental factors? Perhaps the reason why Johnny wants to be a scientist, or why Mary wants to be a pianist, is genetic? Questions two and three are too complex to be dealt with here, so we will look, albeit briefly, at question one: which is the more important – nature or nurture?

How can we take any kind of observed behaviour, sometimes called the phenotype, and assess the degree to which it is determined by genetic causes? There are many ways of doing this. In our type of civilization at the present time, it seems that genetic factors account for over twice as many of the observed phenotypic differences in IQ as do environmental factors. Why specify time and culture? The reason is because heritability is not an absolute number, like the speed of light, but depends on circumstances. This will become obvious on reflection.

Let us assume that among the environmental influences that determine differences in IQ is quality of education. Now imagine two civilizations. In one, all children go to school, all schools are run by the state and teaching is universally good (this would be roughly true in Germany or France). In the other, some children get a very good education, some a poor one and many practically none at all (this would be roughly true in some African countries). Environment clearly plays a much greater part in the second group, and heritability of IQ will be higher in the first group. Anything that makes for equality in a society will tend to raise the heritability of IQ; anything that reduces equality will lower it. A study in Norway illustrates this point well. It compared heritability of scholastic achievement shortly after the war, when inequalities were common, and later on, when egalitarianism was introduced to the school system. Heritability increased considerably from the original to the later condition.

How Do We Measure Heritability?

The first method of measuring heritability makes use of the fact that identical (monozygotic or MZ) twins share 100 per cent of their genes and are indeed identical from the point of view of heredity. Any differences in IQ must therefore be due to environment. We sometimes find identical twins who have been separated at birth, or shortly afterwards, and brought up separately. When we measure their IQs as adults, they turn out to be very similar indeed. Nature, it seems, is over twice as powerful as nurture.

Secondly, MZ twins are not the only kind; there are also dizygotic (DZ) twins, sometimes called fraternal twins, who share, on average, only 50 per cent of their heredity. (To produce MZ twins, one fertilized egg splits in two to produce two identical individuals; to produce DZ twins, two eggs are simultaneously fertilized by two sperms, producing two individuals no more alike genetically than brothers and sisters born on different occasions.) If heredity is important, MZ twins should be much closer to each other in respect to IQ than DZ twins, and indeed that is so; MZ twins are roughly twice as similar as DZ twins.

Our third test is to take babies adopted at birth and test them when they are in their teens. We can then compare their IQs with those of their biological parents (who provide their heredity) and those of their adoptive parents (who provide their environment). Results have shown that children's IQs are much closer to those of their true parents than those of their adoptive parents. Indeed, as the child gets older, his or her IQ grows increasingly similar to that of the true parents and decreasingly similar to that of the adoptive parents. This, too, is powerful evidence.

A fourth method is to look at similarities in IQ between different family relations. On genetic grounds, we would expect degree of consanguinity to correspond to degree of similarity in IQ. Siblings (brothers and sisters) should, for example, be as similar as father or mother and son or daughter. Cousins should show much less similarity, and so forth. Investigation has shown that prediction from the genetic hypothesis is borne out quite precisely: the closer the blood relationship, the greater the IQ similarity.

Methods five and six are closely related, being the opposite sides of the same coin. When parents are related, such as in the case of marriages between cousins, we tend to get 'inbreeding depression' because of the presence of bad alleles (one of two alternative Mendelian characters in similar sites on the chromosomes of the parents). This should (and does) lead to lower IQs in the children so afflicted. Conversely, 'heterosis' refers to the getting together of parents from different races, such as Caucasian and Oriental. Here we would expect what is sometimes called 'hybrid vigour', an improvement of IQ. Indeed, this is what has been found.

The seventh method uses an environmental manipulation. If environment (or rather, differences in environment) is important in producing differences in IQ, then if we could reduce these differences in environment to an absolute minimum, we should at the same time reduce to a minimum differences in IQ of the children brought up in this environment. In other words, all the children should have similar IQs. Two sorts of studies have investigated the effects of such environmental manipulation. In one, a study is made of children committed to an orphanage at a very early age. All grew up in conditions as similar as it is humanly possible to produce: same food, same teachers, same everything. Yet differences in IQ are hardly smaller in this group than in the outside world. Another study looked at children brought up in a suburb of Warsaw under communist rule, where all the families lived in identical houses, earned identical amounts, where children went to identical schools, and everything was regimented to be as identical as possible. Here, again, differences in IQ remained as large as in the free Western world.

The final method is particularly important. The results are essential to a proper understanding of what we really mean when we say that differences are largely genetic in origin, and what the consequences of such a state of affairs may be socially. Figure 2 illustrates what most people think is implied by such hereditarian notions: bright parents have bright children; dull parents have dull children; average parents have average children. In other words, a caste society in which every child's future is already determined from the beginning. But this is not how the genes work. Genetics teaches us that what we actually get is regression to the mean: the children of bright parents are bright on the average, but less so than their parents. Similarly, the children of dull parents are dull, but less so than their parents.

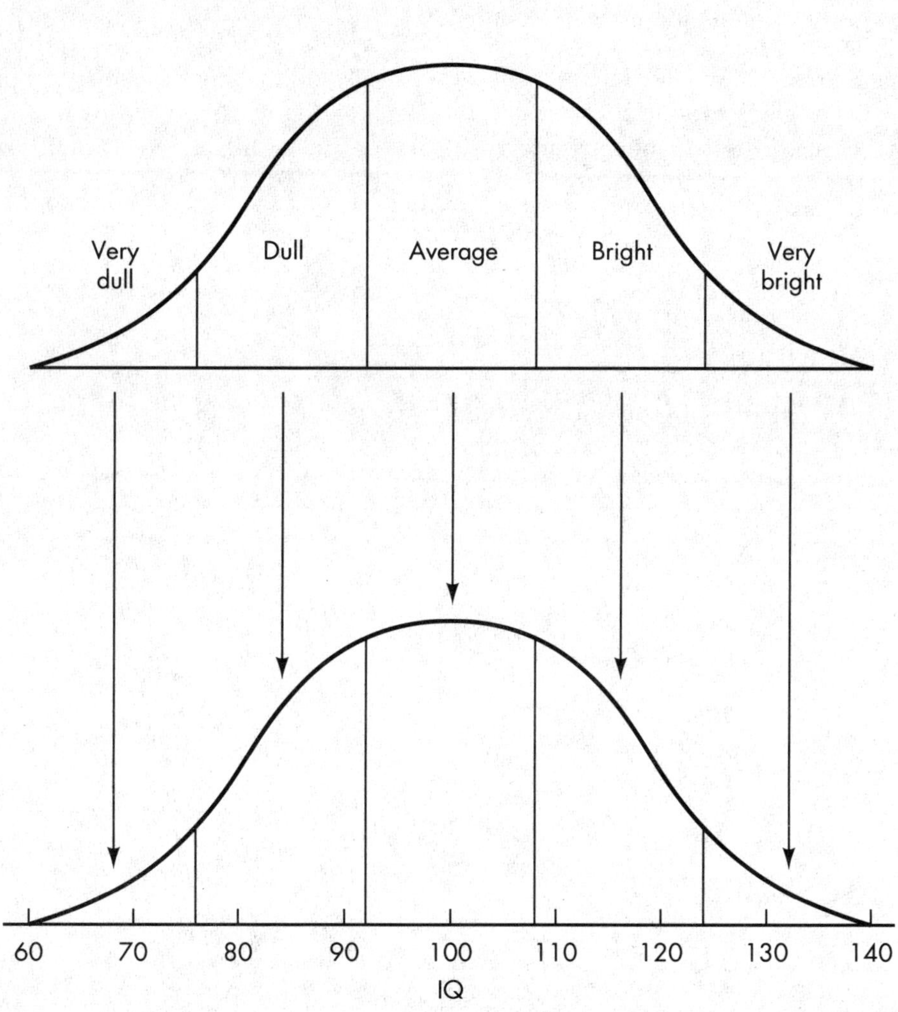

Figure 2. How most people perceive the inheritance of intelligence.

Figure 3, shows what is actually happening. There is amazing variety in the IQs of the offspring of a given set of parents. Of the children of very bright parents, one might be very bright, two bright and one average. Genes segregate in a different way for each conception, hence children of a given couple can differ widely in IQ. Regression to the mean is counterbalanced by the spreading of the children of average parents who can sometimes be very bright, sometimes very dull but, on average, have an IQ of between 90 and 110.

Thus regression to the mean, which is exactly what genetic theory predicts, creates a socially mobile society, with the bright going up in the world and the dull going down. This has been found to be true even within a given family, where

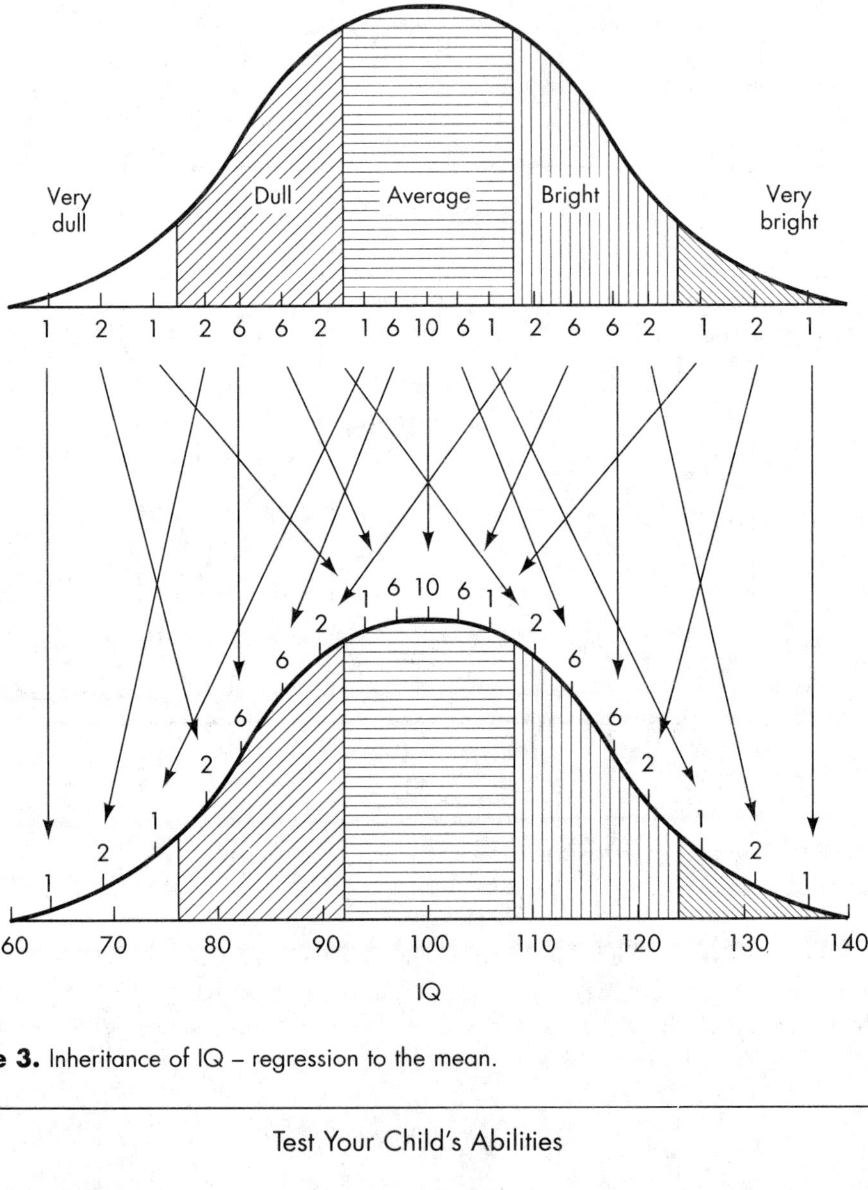

Figure 3. Inheritance of IQ – regression to the mean.

environmental conditions are very similar for all children. Socio-economic success is a function of IQ. Genetics does not create a caste system; regression to the mean is responsible for social mobility, which is the characteristic feature of modern capitalistic society.

What is most impressive about these proofs of the importance of genetic factors in producing differences in IQ is the fact that they all agree, when properly quantified, on the relative importance of nature and nurture. In modern Western societies, roughly 70 per cent of these differences are due to genetic causes and 30 per cent to environmental factors. There are many technical problems and difficulties in all this work, and many large-scale studies are required before we can be sure. Yet as early as 1941, there were enough studies to enable Professor Woodworth, an eminent American psychologist, to arrive at the figure of 70 per cent nature versus 30 per cent environment. Surveying the much more extensive literature recently, together with a professional geneticist, we arrived at the same figure. (We did not take into account the data published by Professor Cyril Burt which have been criticized as possibly fraudulent; there is so much evidence that any one person's contribution makes no noticeable difference to the final outcome.)

These eight proofs should be enough to convince anybody of the importance of genetic factors in the creation of IQ differences. One further point, however, needs to be made. What has been said is true of groups, such as people living in England born between 1916 and 1936, but it does not apply to individuals. You cannot say that your son's, or your daughter's, IQ is determined to the extent of 70 per cent by heredity and 30 per cent by environment. Such a statement is meaningless. Estimates of heritability are always derived from groups, and applicable only to groups; they are in effect averages, and as such do not carry any meaning for individuals.

Intelligence – or Intelligences?

As we have seen, Galton upheld a view of a single cognitive (mental) ability, and Binet offered a dozen or so different abilities. This difference was taken up by Charles Spearman in London, who took Galton's part, and Leo Thurstone in Chicago, who took Binet's part. However, where Galton and Binet had been content with an inconclusive intellectual argument, Spearman and Thurstone adopted an experimental and statistical approach. It would be going well beyond the limits of a book like this to go into the mysteries of factor analysis and matrix algebra, but the underlying principles are clear enough.

Let us start with Galton's theory that there is one general ability underlying all cognitive activity. If Smith has more of this ability than Jones, he will tend to do better than Jones on *all* types of cognitive problems. This is the principle of the 'positive manifold' – if you give any number of IQ test items to any random selection of people, then those who do well on any one test will tend to do well on all the others, and those who do badly on any one test will tend to do badly on all the others. The 'tend to' is quantitatively expressed in terms of correlations. Perfect agreement is expressed as 1 in correlational terms, no agreement at all as 0. What has been found in hundreds of experiments is that all such correlations are positive, thus lending support to the principle. This was Spearman's original point, and so far so good. He then went one step further, looking at the *pattern* of correlations.

Why are these observed correlations not all equal to 1? Chance plays a large part but, in addition, different test items involve different amounts of intelligence. Other factors, like specific knowledge or preference for verbal or numerical problems, also play a part. This is useful to know, as it guides us in the selection of 'good' test items. Those which correlate highest with all others are obviously better tests of the intelligence we are trying to measure than items correlating poorly with the rest. This fact should give us a particular pattern of intercorrelations; a matrix of rank one, as a mathematician would express it. Spearman claimed that his results produced just such a matrix of intercorrelations.

Thurstone carried out one of the largest studies ever. Using 56 different tests on 240 students, he calculated all the intercorrelations and then used a complex statistical procedure to demonstrate that there was no general factor of intelligence, rather a number of what he called 'primary factors', or special abilities, such as verbal intelligence, numerical intelligence, visuo-spatial intelligence and memory. Thurstone seemed to have vindicated Binet's original theory – that there are many intelligences, not just one single intelligence.

On reanalysing Thurstone's results, it was found that Spearman and Thurstone were both right. There was evidence of a strong general factor of intelligence (labelled 'g' by Spearman), but there was also evidence for Thurstone's 'primaries'. This was soon acknowledged to be true, if somewhat reluctantly, by both Spearman and Thurstone, and practically everyone now agrees that, while there is a powerful factor of general intelligence, there also exist special abilities over and above 'g'. These special factors are very important and may often determine a person's occupational choices.

Sir Aubrey Lewis, the then head of the Institute of Psychiatry, commissioned a researcher to set a battery of tests for incoming students. He wanted to follow them up to see if it was possible to predict who would make a good psychiatrist. Thurstone's primary ability tests were administered, and the students were expected to do reasonably well on all. The result was nothing of the sort. They scored brilliantly on the verbal tests and abysmally on the numerical ones. This makes sense when one considers the kind of work psychiatrists do: talking endlessly with patients, interpreting apparently insignificant verbal nuances, telling patients the 'meaning' of their dreams. Research in psychiatry at that time used only the most primitive statistics, if any at all. Small wonder that the profession attracted medical students with high verbal and low numerical abilities. Overall, their intelligence was no different from that of most medical students.

Studies of students of physics and astronomy have given exactly the opposite results. They are brilliant on numerical tests, abysmal on verbal ones. This ties up very well with professional requirements – they need to master extremely complex mathematics, but need hardly any verbal ability as their results are expressed in formulae. Physicists and astronomers are famous for their inability to express themselves in words, with a few outstanding examples! But, overall, physicists and astronomers score highly, better than the group of psychiatry students.

Since those days, much research has been carried out to identify the major primaries, and some two dozen have now been identified and measured. John Carroll has published an 800-page book on Human Cognitive Abilities, describing them and discussing their statistical respectability. There are five abilities that appear to be the most important in occupational choice and that seem to matter most in schoolwork and at university: 'verbal', 'numerical', 'visuo-spatial', 'perceptual' and 'reasoning'. These abilities form the basis of the tests in this book. The names given to the various primaries or special abilities provide some idea of what they are about. The 'Examples' section which precedes the tests demonstrates the kind of items that are used to measure the five primaries involved, and gives the child a chance to become acquainted with the type of item he or she is likely to encounter.

The classification used involves differences in type of material used: verbal ability uses words to state the problems to be solved while numerical ability uses numbers. Other differences involve different mental processes: reasoning problems involve reasoning (obviously!) while memory problems require the subject to remember and later reproduce verbal, numerical or figural material he or she has learned. Consider verbal and visuo-spatial ability. What is involved is (a) differences in the materials used and (b) differences in the mental processes involved. Here are two typical examples of a verbal test called the synonym and antonym test:

Which of these words means the same as *apathy*?

1. antagonism 2. apartheid 3. passivity 4. apex

Which of these words means the opposite to *frivolous*?

1. frisky 2. serious 3. frightened 4. grandiose

Now compare this with a test of visuo-spatial ability:

Which of these shapes cannot be rotated to resemble the others?

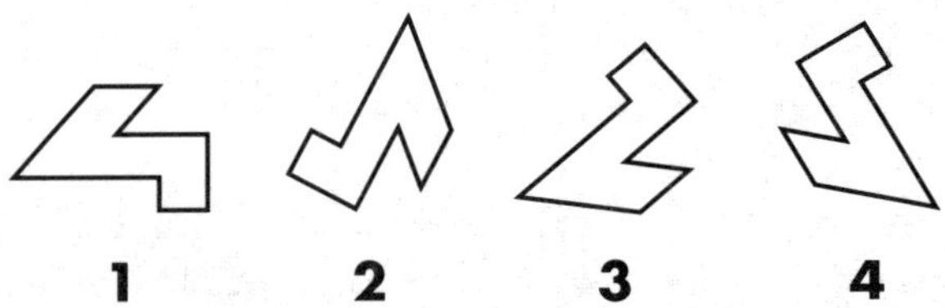

The answer is number 3, as you have to turn it over for it to be on the same plane as the others. So in the first case the material is verbal, in the second it is figural. Mental manipulation in the first case is logical: does A mean the same or the opposite of B? In the second, it is a question of rotating the figure in your mind's eye, and involves imagery. These are clearly different abilities, exercised on different materials. It may seem miraculous that two very different tests correlate together, but they do! Facts such as these establish the 'positive manifold' and support the theory of general intelligence.

There are still one or two psychologists who believe in separate 'intelligences'. In his book *Frames of Mind*, H. Gardner maintains belief in separate types of intelligence: linguistic, musical, logical and mathematical, spatial, bodily-kinaesthetic and personal (the ability to understand oneself and other people).

Unfortunately, he produces no tests to measure the musical, kinaesthetic and personal intelligences, and the other three are known not to be independent, and are represented by tests given in this book. These six 'intelligences' are all primaries, but not independent ones; they are most likely to correlate together to give a measure of general intelligence.

Problems of Measurement

Given that in addition to 'g' or general intelligence we also have various special abilities, how can we measure all of these? Consider 'g' first. We can do one of three things:

- We can select test items that (a) are good measures of 'g', i.e. correlate highly with all other items and (b) do not correlate highly with measures of the various special abilities. These items thus measure just 'g', and little else.

- We can incorporate items in our test that measure all the different special abilities (or at least most of them); by adding them all together to obtain a score, we ensure that none of the special abilities is given special prominence or importance, so that all that remains is the general ability they all have in common.

- We can give separate tests for each of the major special abilities and score each separately to obtain a measure of verbal ability, numerical ability, visuo-spatial ability, etc. This gives us a profile of abilities for each person, with the average of all the special abilities tested giving us a good estimate of his or her 'g'.

Option three is the best, but the most time-consuming. And why do we need a profile? Consider two children, Fred and John. Figure 4 shows their IQs for the five special abilities tested in this book. Fred is destined to be a scientist, John a psychiatrist. John's verbal IQ is 140, but his numerical IQ is only 90. Fred's verbal IQ is 100, but his numerical IQ is 140. They do not differ much on the other three tests. Averaging their scores gives them both a general IQ of 118, which means that both will be able to go to university, but that Fred would probably do very poorly if he studied English, history or philosophy, but would probably do well in mathematics, physics or astronomy. John, on the other hand, would probably do quite well in the literary subjects, but would probably fail in scientific or mathematical subjects. Neither would be likely to turn out a genius at whatever he undertook to study: an IQ of 118 is not really adequate for Ph.D. work.

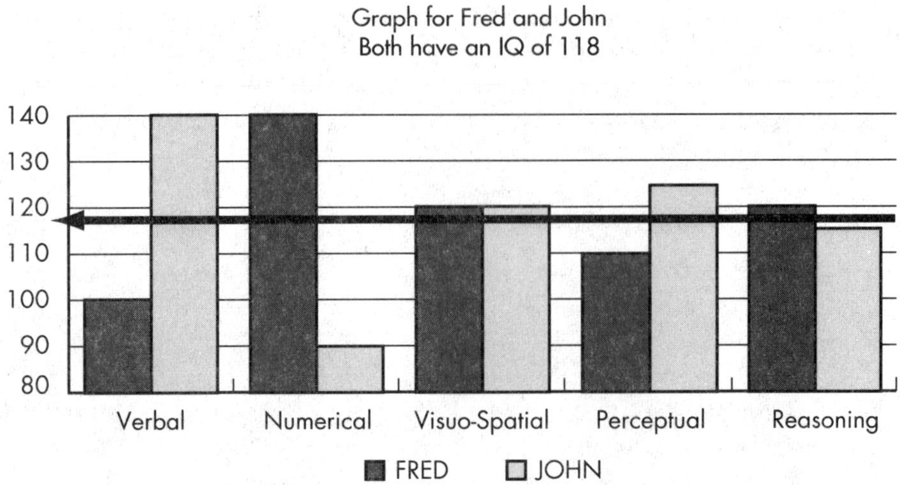

Figure 4. Profile of abilities for two children, Fred and John.

Which is more important: the general IQ or the special abilities? No overall answer is possible; it all depends on circumstances and the actual scores. If all your abilities cluster round a certain level, so that the scores are all just above or below the given 'g' score, then the general IQ tells you all there is to know. But if one or other of the special abilities is way above or below the mean, then the general IQ does not provide enough information, and the knowledge of one's special intellectual strengths and weaknesses becomes much more important. For Fred and John, knowing their high and low scores would be vital, their general IQ level much less so.

Much depends on circumstances. At school a child is likely to compete with a wide variety of children of all different degrees of ability. Here, particularly in primary school, 'g' is especially important. In secondary school, some selection will probably have taken place so that the child is less differentiated from his or her classmates by general intelligence. Here special abilities begin to play an important role, particularly when the child has to decide which subjects to study for examinations.

This trend continues at university. Everyone who is accepted by a good university is bright enough to succeed in his or her studies; special abilities determine to a large extent just which subjects would be the most likely to produce a successful outcome. Past successes and failures are a good guide, but objective test results may be more reliable in such a situation. Many youngsters take English or history, because so many others take these subjects, and not because of any special liking for them or any special verbal ability. There may be an unrecognized numerical ability struggling to get out, and a subject like psychology, with its large statistical underpinnings, might be much more suitable. (On the other hand many students choose psychology in ignorance of the large part statistics play in psychological research, and are sorely disappointed that their numerical deficiencies are mercilessly exposed.) Universities should routinely carry out psychometric testing on all prospective students and discuss results with them prior to any subject choices being made; unfortunately nothing of the sort is being done in the UK. In the USA, the SAT (Scholastic Aptitude Test) is a required admission test for most good universities; this has a verbal and a numerical section, separately scored, so that candidate and university know where they stand.

Schools, too, should routinely carry out ability testing in order to be able to advise children about which courses to take, and where they have the best chance to shine. Such tests would also help teachers to appreciate the weaknesses of some children, the strengths of others; to make allowances for abilities that are lacking, and to concentrate on abilities amply present. Teachers consistently overlook high abilities and fail to take into account low abilities. Indeed, without proper testing, there is no way a teacher, particularly when confronting a large class, can hope to recognize such complex ability patterns. Hopeful beliefs in egalitarianism do not help in the recognition of the large intellectual differences that undoubtedly exist. To be aware of these differences, and to capitalize on them, should be one of the prime tasks of teachers. In their absence, parents may fulfil that function with the help of this book.

These, however, are not the only problems in measurement. Right from the beginning of IQ testing, psychologists and educators have faced the question of speed versus power. You can test IQ along two quite different lines. One way of constructing a test is by using problems of increasing difficulty, so that even the dullest can solve the easier problems, but only the brightest can solve the most difficult. A test constructed along these lines is called a 'power' test, because it attempts to ascertain the intellectual power of the person tested. Another way is to have a large number of relatively easy problems, easy enough for most if not all candidates to solve given enough time. The test is timed, however, so that even the brightest cannot solve all the problems in the time given. What we appear to be measuring here is the speed of mental functioning, and it has often been suggested that speed and power are separate qualities, with speed reflecting some more superficial mental quality. But any such conclusion would be incorrect.

Reaction Time

The results of power tests and speed tests correlate together so highly that there appears to be little meaningful distinction. This brings us back to Galton's theory, and his suggestion that intelligence might be measured by means of reaction time (RT) testing. Figure 5 illustrates the apparatus that is used to carry out these very simple tests. The subject is presented with a console on which there are eight small lights arranged in a semicircle. In front of each light is a button. The lights go on and off randomly, with only one lighting up at any one time. The subject has to press the button next to each light as soon as it comes on, moving his or her finger from the 'home' button to the target as quickly as possible. The time interval between the light coming on and the subject pressing the right button is the reaction time. Experiments have shown that reaction-time speed does correlate with IQ, as Galton predicted, and it correlates equally well with tests of speed as it does with tests of power.

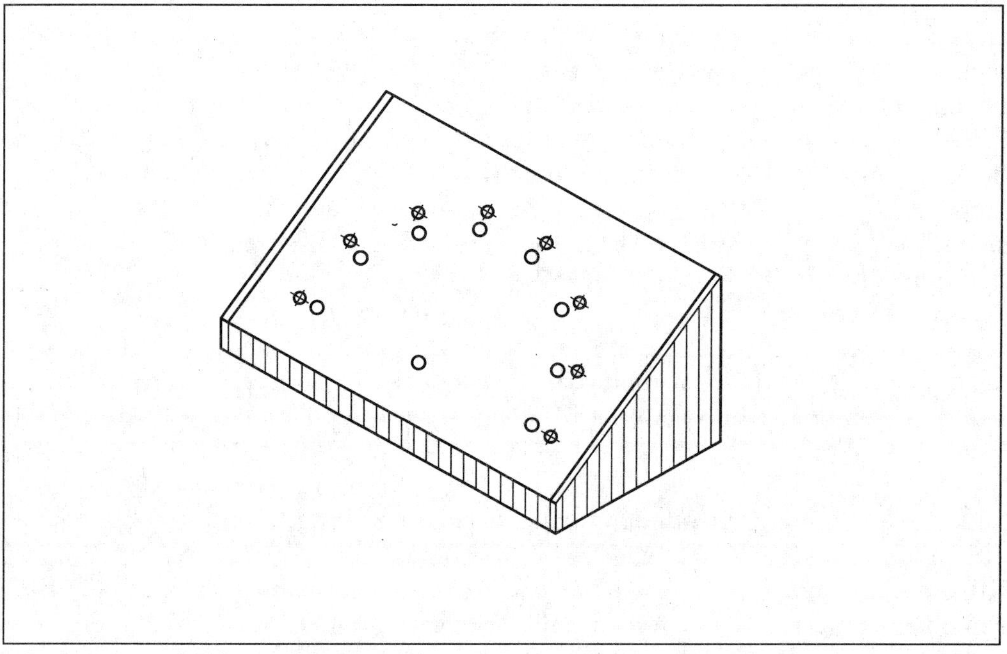

Figure 5. Apparatus to measure reaction time/movement time. Push buttons are indicated by circles; green jewelled lights by circled crosses. The 'home' button is in the lower centre, six inches from each response button.

Inspection Time

Somewhat different are tests of inspection time (IT), which measure the time taken to perceive a very simple figure. Typically, two lines are exposed for a very short time (100 milliseconds or less), one of which is much shorter than the other; your score is the shortest exposure time which enables you to say correctly whether the line on the right or the line on the left is longer. Here, too, the shorter the time required, the higher your IQ. Taking together a battery of RT and IT tests gives you a score that correlates with an IQ test almost as highly as one IQ test correlates with another.

Findings such as these support theories like Galton's, according to which differences in intelligence are mediated by differences in the speed of mental processing, i.e. the speed with which nervous impulses circulate in the cortex and transmit information. This belief is supported by direct studies of cortical activity, where cortical events are recorded on the electroencephalograph. Here, too, quick responses to elementary stimuli (a flash of light, a sound) are found to be correlated with high IQ. Power tests work because speedy cortical responses enable complex responses to be performed within a reasonable space of time; if your responses are slow, you will never get your act together!

Most modern tests combine aspects of speed and power. Items are devised to incorporate levels of difficulty from easy to medium-difficult, or even very difficult, but the test has to be completed in a given period of time. Almost the only tests not having a time limit are some that are individually administered. Most tests now are group tests that can be administered to groups of children or adults sitting in a large room, and supervised by a teacher or psychologist who times the test (or the various parts of the test). Individually administered tests are usually given in circumstances where a specially accurate result is required, and where there may be problems of test anxiety or malingering. Thus psychiatric patients are usually tested individually, as are prisoners in cases where mental defect is pleaded. Individual testing is usually more accurate and informative, but much more expensive.

Fluid and Crystallized Ability

Individual testing, as in the Binet tests, has led to an important distinction. Some of the tests are verbal; in other words, they require the use of language in the solution. Others are non-verbal or performance tests. The child might be given a kind of jigsaw puzzle to fit together; or the test might consist of wooden blocks with different designs on each side. These have to be fitted together in such a way that a design put before the child is duplicated. This differentiation is important because it leads to the measurement of two somewhat different classes of abilities often referred to as fluid and crystallized ability. These differ in the following way.

Intelligence may be thought of and defined as a dispositional variable, something enabling us to reason, think abstractly, solve problems, learn new material quickly, and so forth. This meaning is intended when we talk about fluid ability. Fluid means simply that this underlying mental capacity can be used in many different ways and for many different purposes. It would enable you to learn any language, mathematics, chemistry, history, literature or any other subject.

Intelligence can also be seen, however, as the possession of a certain amount of knowledge. You have learned Latin, rather than Russian; you have become proficient in mathematics, rather than history. You have exchanged your fluid ability for acquired knowledge; in other words, your fluid ability has become crystallized. Fluid ability is potential; crystallized ability is actual. Fluid ability is best measured by non-verbal or performance tests; crystallized ability by verbal tests. One of the best verbal tests is the vocabulary test, measuring the extent of your word knowledge; clearly this is crystallized ability, a measure of acquired knowledge. The brighter you are (fluid ability), the greater the vocabulary you have acquired, other things being equal. Hence the vocabulary test is one of the best measures of IQ. Fluid ability causes and predicts crystallized ability; it is the more fundamental, but for many purposes it may be useful to have a measure of crystallized ability. Why?

Consider the tasks facing a psychologist who has to select, from a much larger group of applicants, those who are to be accepted for entry into a prestigious grammar school or a leading university. His choice should maximize the number of students passing, preferably at a high level, and minimize the number of failures and dropouts. Fluid ability has been found again and again to be a most useful predictor, but a person may have a high degree of fluid ability without possessing other important qualities such as persistence, the habit of working hard and the love of knowledge which produces strong motivation. An indirect measure of such additional qualities is given by a test of crystallized ability; this measures acquired knowledge, and the acquisition of such knowledge is an indication of persistence, hard work and motivation. Without these extra qualities, fluid ability would not have turned into crystallized ability. Hence, in choosing our students, a test of crystallized ability may give us a better prediction than a test of fluid ability. Best of all would be a test combining both, and the leading individual tests give equal importance to fluid and crystallized ability, and provide separate scores for both, as well as an overall, combined IQ.

Crystallized ability measures are not the same as tests of scholastic achievement which are designed to test knowledge of certain areas that have been covered by the syllabus. However bright you are in terms of fluid ability, you will not do well in such a test unless you have been exposed to teaching geared to that curriculum. Scholastic achievement tests are too closely tied to specific teaching and knowledge to be acceptable as IQ tests. Crystallized ability tests are much more general, like the vocabulary test. Schools do not teach vocabulary; you acquire it by a kind of osmosis – by hearing words used by other people, by reading newspapers and magazines, by listening to the radio or television. There are many sources of vocabulary intake, and the brighter you are the more you take in. Hence the vocabulary test is a very good measure of IQ; the crystallized ability it represents is a good mirror of the fluid ability that enables you to acquire the knowledge of words it measures.

Can You Increase Your Child's IQ?

If IQ is so very important in education, occupation, and life generally, and if IQ is to some extent (say 30 per cent) determined by environmental factors, then should we not be able to increase it to a considerable extent? Theoretically, if we start with children at the bottom of the environmental ladder (deprived children who have to cope with factors such as poor schooling, bad surroundings and malnutrition and non-caring parents) and gave them the best environment possible, then we should be able to increase their IQ by 30 points or so. Several psychologists have claimed to have succeeded in doing just that.

There have been many stories of increases in IQ of 30 or even 40 points, many of which are analysed in Herman Spitz's book *The Raising of Intelligence*. Spitz concludes that there is simply no evidence for any such wondrous increases in IQ. You may have read about some of these in the papers, such as the recent 'Milwaukee Miracle', but you are unlikely to have read about the usual final debacle, where scientific criticism shows the weaknesses in such projects, and sadly concludes that at best there are some relatively small and evanescent effects. The media splashed the original claims all over their pages, because that is 'news' but hardly ever mention the fact that rigorous examinations of the claims has shown them to be unfounded. One 'miracle' claimant was sent to prison for misappropriation of research funds – the whole story is full of tragicomedy.

One important point should be mentioned here. You get an advantage in IQ testing by just doing one or two tests before taking the crucial test – say a school entrance examination. This is due to test sophistication – you are familiar with the test-taking requirements, and know what is expected of you. You know the typical questions you are likely to encounter, and do not have to waste time reading instructions. You know better what sorts of problems to go for, and which to leave to the end. By practising on several tests, you can raise your (apparent) IQ by something like 10 points. It is for this reason that psychologists have always advised schools to give several IQ tests in advance of an important selection test; in this way all the children start on a fair and equal footing. But most schools plead poverty, and refuse to carry out such testing.

There is much you can do for your child, such as being interested in the child's educational progress, encouraging academic interests, providing books, journals and papers, restricting television viewing, supervising homework, discussing problems of art, politics and ethics and generally being an intelligent parent for the growing child. Although this may help to increase the child's verbal and crystallized ability, it is not likely to do much for his or her fluid ability. But every little helps!

So far we have talked about the 30 per cent of intelligence that is environmentally conditioned. But if IQ is largely biological, might it not be worthwhile to look for biological methods of improvement? Recent studies have shown that some children (perhaps one in three or four) respond strongly to vitamin and mineral supplements, increasing their IQ by quite sizeable amounts. This improvement occurs only in children whose diet is lacking in vitamins and minerals, such as children who eat 'junk' foods full of fat and sugar. There are now 10 studies that have given supportive results.

In all these studies, the improvement was always in fluid (non-verbal) ability, as one would expect; it was never in crystallized (verbal) ability. Crystallized ability is what has been learned in the past, and not likely to be affected by nutritional supplementation. But fluid ability affects the ease of learning new material, or reasoning well, or working quickly on mental tasks, and that could be affected by supplements.

Little is known about the best age at which to give nutritional supplements, but common sense suggests the earlier the better. Strongest effects are expected when the pregnant mother is given the supplements; babies and young children are then most likely to benefit. As children get older, the benefits of supplementation diminish. At the age of 12, there is still a very noticeable effect, but at 18, there is very little. Not enough is known to be definite about this matter. Results last for at least a year; whether they are permanent or not is not yet known.

Where Do Your Child's Talents Lie?

Can we predict who will do well at what? There are two ways of looking at this issue: occupational selection and vocational guidance. These are in a sense complementary. Occupational selection tries to find the best candidate to fill a particular position. Most employers use an interview, although there is a great deal of evidence that interviews give little worthwhile information on job-related skills and personal qualities other than what is already contained on the candidate's CV. One famous study used 12 experienced interviewers to interview 57 prospective candidates for a job. The interviewers all made their recommendations and there was absolutely no agreement between them; the same man might appear at the top of our interviewer's list, at the bottom of another's and somewhere in the middle for the third! Interviewing is too subjective to be valid, and many studies have shown that interviewing predictions are highly unlikely to succeed better than chance. In this they are on a par with other non-scientific methods of selection, such as astrology and graphology, both thoroughly discredited.

Tests are more effective than interviews. It has been calculated that, through successful use of tests to select the best candidates for its varied services, the US government saves 16 billion dollars a year – more than the annual general income of many countries! Whenever interviews have been pinned against test selection, the latter has always won – handsomely. This is because we can objectively investigate the abilities required for a given job, construct or select tests of those abilities and choose those applicants possessing those abilities to the greatest extent. There are problems, but they have not proved insurmountable.

Vocational guidance starts with the individual, and attempts to guide him or her into an appropriate job, occupation or profession, depending on his or her abilities. This is much more difficult. In occupational selection you have one job to deal with, and one set of tests; in vocational guidance you have an infinitude of possible jobs, and hence a large number of tests – more than you could give any youngster in a reasonable number of hours. Is it possible to do this successfully?

A number of years ago, the National Institute of Industrial Psychology (sadly now defunct) rigged up an experiment comparing a control group of male school-leavers who received only the standard advice of a careers officer, with an experimental group receiving advice based on psychological principles from members of the NIIP. The boys were then followed up, and grouped into those who followed the advice given and those who did not. Also noted was the success of the advice in terms of earnings, remaining in the job and job satisfaction. The result was very clear. For the control group, those who followed the teacher's advice did, if anything, less well than those who disregarded it. For the NIIP team, those who followed the advice did much better than those who did not. Clearly vocational guidance is possible, and can be done successfully.

There are problems in all this. The first is that the nature of a job is seldom well specified by the single term used to characterize it. A 'secretary', for example, can refer to an office junior or to a high-flying personal assistant. The second problem is that personality may be as important, or even more so, than ability. If you have high general, numerical and perceptual ability, choosing between being a salesperson or an administrator, for example, may depend on your degree of extraversion rather than on your abilities – salespeople tend to be extraverted; administrators introverted.

These two problems often combine. Take truck-drivers, for instance. If you simply drive a truck each day from London to the same address in Manchester, you need little of any of the five primary abilities, and being introverted might help. But if you take your truck to varying destinations on the continent, you would need high intelligence, verbal ability, numerical ability and perceptual ability. You need to make and change plans depending on circumstances; to keep in mind exchange rates and calculate equivalent prices; to communicate in foreign languages; to talk your way out of difficult situations; to get on with people – all of which requires a certain amount of extraversion. So the term 'trucker' may hide all sorts of differences in actual job description. All of this should be borne in mind when considering the following general suggestion regarding abilities required for certain occupations.

All of the so-called 'professions' demand a high degree of reasoning ability. Lawyers, historians and professors of English and history require good verbal ability, as do psychiatrists and, perhaps, medical practitioners in general. Mathematicians, statisticians, engineers, physicists, chemists and psychologists need high numerical ability, as do actuaries, bank employees, accountants and anyone who has a lot to do with figures. Visuo-spatial ability is more likely to be needed in architects, designers, geometricians, artists and such like. Finally, perceptual ability is needed in jobs where accuracy is important such as for executives, administrators, bank clerks, librarians, accountants and clerical workers. Police, too, have a lot of clerical work to do, and need high perceptual ability.

Salespeople and sales administrators need verbal and numerical ability; travelling salespeople also need visuo-spatial ability (and any others depending on the exact nature of their jobs). People in trades and crafts (mechanics, processing workers, electricians, industrial inspectors) need reasoning and visuo-spatial ability. Skilled agricultural workers need numerical, visuo-spatial and perceptual ability. These examples will hopefully make clear the general principles involved. To use the profile of scores your child gets from this book, get him or her to think and feel him or herself into a possible job or occupation, envisage what he or she will be expected to do, and relate this to the pattern of scoring.

In addition to ability and personality, personal preference has always been found important in making the right choice. Your child's desire to work either with other people or alone; to work in the country or in a town; with machines or with people; to determine his or her own rate of working or to fall in with a given regime – these preferences dictate the sort of work your child will feel happiest with, and should be consulted very seriously. The choice of a career is extremely important yet, like marriage, most people just drift into it. Your child needs any help you can give, and if his or her ability profile helps your child make a sensible choice, we shall be pleased. Even if doing the tests simply encourages your child to give some serious thought to the future, and try to have a look at what is implied in some of the occupations to which he or she is drawn, that would be a good beginning.

Why Measure Intelligence?

People sometimes wonder why we should bother to measure intelligence. There are many reasons, both scientific and practical. The scientific ones are obvious – it is better to know than not to know. The more we know about intelligence, personality, motivation, emotion and other human attributes, the better; knowledge is inherently better than ignorance. We cannot tell what important consequences may flow from the discovery that you can scientifically measure a mental quality, but future generations will reap the benefits of our research.

This is not to say that, even now, there are not many substantial benefits to be derived from the testing of intelligence. We can now tell with certainty that teaching of mixed-ability classes is less successful than teaching of roughly equal-ability classes, and we can select children appropriately. That alone, if only teachers were willing to pay attention to facts rather than to 'political correctness', would justify IQ testing. But we can go further and show that such IQ testing can be justified on humanistic grounds. Selection used to work on the basis of scholastic achievement; children were admitted to prestigious grammar schools on the basis of knowledge acquired during their formative years. But middle-class children had the advantage over working-class children of being sent to better primary schools, having a better home background and environment, being helped in every way to pass the entrance requirements of the grammar schools. IQ tests were originally constructed and introduced as selection devices in the UK in order to equalize chances of better education for working-class children, as far as possible, and evidence shows that they succeeded in doing so. When the use of IQ tests as selection tools was discontinued by a Labour government, the proportion of working-class children in higher education immediately dropped quite drastically. IQ testing is an agent of social justice.

The same is true when we turn to occupational selection. We are all familiar with nepotism, and the principle of 'it is more important whom you know than what you know'. Ability testing is objective, and selects the best person for a given job; there is no question of favouritism here.

IQ testing has transformed the assessment of intelligence from vague guesswork into true measurement; not yet perfect, but already accurate enough for most practical purposes. The effect on intelligence of lead emissions from motor exhausts in inner-cities is small in terms of IQ, but it has been found to be quite definite, depressing the affected child's intelligence. We could never have proved this without the help of IQ tests. Ignorant jibes notwithstanding, IQ testing is scientifically meaningful, socially useful and ethically desirable in eliminating subjectivity in appraisal. Your child can be a beneficiary of what IQ testing has to offer.

Self-testing, as with this book, can be fairly accurate if instructions are followed precisely. Readers of previous, similar volumes have often written to say how similar their IQ came out when tested with the use of the standard tests. With younger children, the test should preferably be administered by an unrelated adult, or by parents or older siblings. If a really accurate result is required, a special individually administered test or set of tests should be chosen, with an experienced psychologist giving the test. The tests in this book should be used as a rough guide, not the final word in your child's pattern of abilities.

How to Use This Book

The main body of this book is divided into two sections: the first contains tests for children aged 10–12; the second contains tests for children aged 13–15. There are five tests in each section designed to evaluate the following abilities: abstract reasoning; numerical; perceptual; verbal and visuo-spatial. Each test contains 40 separate items. The correct answers are given at the end of each part. A graph at the back of the book enables you to translate your score into an IQ.

Each test should be timed for 30 minutes. Your child should not be allowed to time him or herself. Tell your child to attempt each test item but to go on to the next one if he or she gets stuck as the items are not in order of difficulty. Your child should check each answer; he or she may be on the right track, but there may be a mistake in figuring it out or in writing it down. As there are some letter sequences, it may be useful for your child to write down the letters of the alphabet in advance to help count the position in a sequence. Give your child a pencil and a piece of paper ready for calculations. Before beginning each test your child should have a good look at the list of examples relevant to that section.

The tests will give you an approximate idea of what your child's IQ is; do not take it too seriously. Self-testing is not recommended when the result is important; if you want a very accurate figure you should contact an experienced psychologist and arrange for your child to be given an individual test. Above all, the tests are meant to give your child an idea of how IQ test items are constructed, how to do the tests and how to score them. It may help if in future your child is called upon to do a test in a selection situation where the results matter.

Examples

Abstract Reasoning Examples

1: What is the next number?

1 2 3 4 ( )

Answer: 5

2: What is the next letter?

A B C D ( )

Answer: E

3: Is the final sentence TRUE or FALSE?

All apples are jugs and all penguins are apples. Therefore all penguins are jugs.

(TRUE) (FALSE)

Answer: TRUE

4: Is the final sentence TRUE or FALSE?

Adam is taller than Amanda. Anthony is taller than Adam. Therefore Anthony is taller than Amanda.

(TRUE) (FALSE)

Answer: TRUE

5: Insert the number of the next symbol in the series in box 'D'.

A	B	C	D	1	2	3	4
<	>	<	☐	>	^	<	%

Answer: 1

6: Insert the number of the missing symbol.

*	@	+
+	*	@
@	+	( )

1	2	3	4
*	@	+	&

Answer: 1

7: There is a rule which makes 'A' become 'B'. Which symbol will 'C' become if it follows the same rule?

A	B	C	1	2	3	4	5
[	]	(	!	=	)	{	>

Answer: 3

Numerical Examples

1: Insert the numbers into the equation so that the equation is correct.

1, 2, 3, 4   **(+) - (+) = 4**

Answer: (3 + 4) – (1 + 2) = 4

2: Insert the missing number.

1	**2**	**3**
4	**5**	**6**
5	**3**	**( )**

Answer: 1. All columns add up to 10.

3: Insert the missing number.

1

( )   **2**

7   **3**

6   **4**

5

Answer: 8

4: Insert the missing number.

1	**3**	**4**
[6]	**[12]**	**[ ]**
2 3	**4 5**	**5 6**

Answer: 15. Add the numbers on the outside of the rectangle to get the inside figure.

5: Fill in the spaces in the table.

Football Match Attendance

	Saturday	Sunday	Wednesday	Total
Adult	1	2	3	( )
Child	4	5	6	( )
Total	5	7	9	( )

Answers: Adult 6, Child 15, Total 21

6: Fill in the spaces in the table so that all rows add up to 20.

1	2	3	4	( )
5	8	2	1	( )
4	5	8	2	( )

Answers: top row 10, middle row 4, bottom row 1

7: Add two of the numbers below to get 17. No combination of numbers can be used more than once.

1	2	3	4	5	6	7	8	9

Answer: 8 + 9

Perceptual Examples

1: Using the key below, underline the set of numbers which matches the set of symbols.

1	2	3	4	5	6	7	8	9
%	#	=	$	<	@	!	)	>

	%	#	=	$	<
a.	1	2	3	4	5
b.	9	8	7	6	5
c.	5	6	7	2	1

Answer: a

2: Each set of symbols in the code column represents a word in the word line. The same symbol represents the same letter in each question. In the translation column, write the words represented by each code.

words: ABET, BEEP, DEEP

code	translation
+ = = $	( )
£ = = $	( )
(+ = @	( )

Answers: top BEEP, middle DEEP, bottom ABET

3: Are these two words spelt the SAME or DIFFERENTLY?

MOUSE	MOUSE
(SAME)	**(DIFFERENTLY)**

Answer: SAME

4: Are these two numbers the SAME or DIFFERENT?

12345	12345
(SAME)	**(DIFFERENT)**

Answer: SAME

5: In the key below, a letter stands for each number. Swop the numbers for the letters to solve the equation.

0	**1**	**2**	**3**	**4**	**5**	**6**	**7**	**8**	**9**
T	**S**	**R**	**Q**	**P**	**O**	**N**	**M**	**L**	**K**

ST + R + Q = ( )

Answer: 15

6: Which of the four numbered symbols is the same as the symbol on the left?

&	**1**	**2**	**3**	**4**
	$	**£**	**&**	*****

Answer: 3

7: Underline all consonants followed by a vowel and all vowels followed by a consonant.

A B C A E R F G E

Answer: A, C, E, G

8: Underline all even numbers followed by an odd number and all odd numbers followed by an even number.

1 2 3 9 4 3 1 7 2 6

Answer: 1, 2, 9, 4, 7

Verbal Examples

1: Do the following words have the SAME or a DIFFERENT meaning?

BIG LARGE

(SAME) (DIFFERENT)

Answer: SAME

2: Fill in the missing letters so the words mean the same as the definition.

Midday meal

L _ N _ H

Answer: LUNCH

3: Which two phrases are the closest in meaning?

a. Have the same problem.

b. Be in the same boat.

c. Feel in the swim.

d. Time and tide wait for no man.

Answer: a and b

4: Each item in column (c) belongs either to column (a) or to column (b). Underline which belongs to (a) and which belongs to (b).

a	b	c		
JANUARY	**DIVIDE**	**OCTOBER**	**a**	**b**
MARCH	**ADD**	**MULTIPLY**	**a**	**b**
MAY	**SUBTRACT**	**AUGUST**	**a**	**b**
		FEBRUARY	**a**	**b**

Answer: October a, Multiply b, August a, February a

5: Underline the odd one out.

a. CAR
b. BOAT
c. SPONGE
d. FERRY

Answer: SPONGE

6: What is the following anagram ?

ROWK ( )

Answer: WORK

7: Is the following jumbled sentence TRUE or FALSE?

GREEN GRASS IS

Answer: TRUE

8: Make as many words as you can from

FRUIT.

Answers: FUR, FIR, FIT, RUT, RIFT, TURF

Visuo-spatial Examples

1: All blocks below are the same size and shape. Decide how many other blocks each block is touching and write this number in the table. Faces or sides touching count but corners do not.

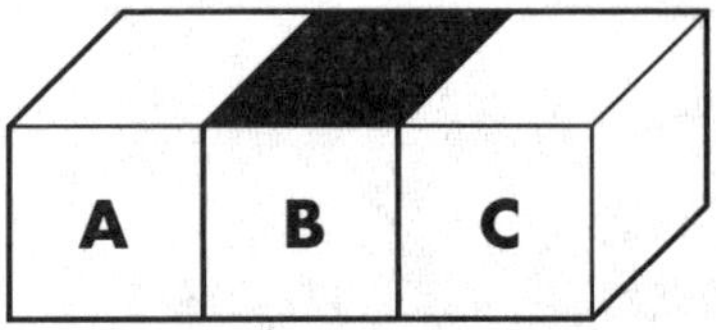

A	
B	
C	

Answer: A 1, B 2, C 1

2: Each side of the two cubes has a different design. If the cubes are rotated, will they be the SAME or DIFFERENT?

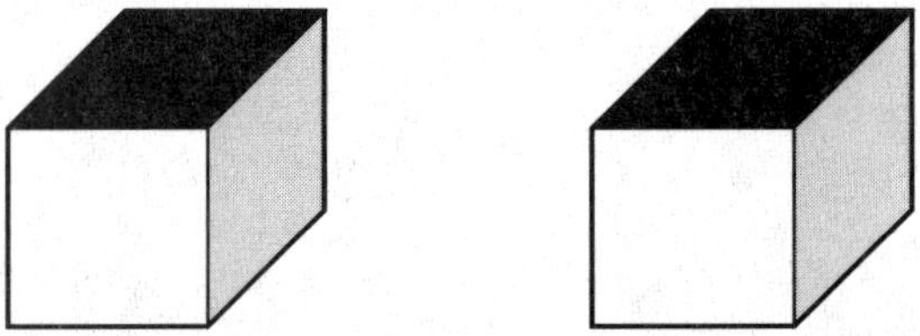

(SAME) **(DIFFERENT)**

Answer: SAME

3: Underline whether the two diagrams show the SAME side of the card or the OPPOSITE side.

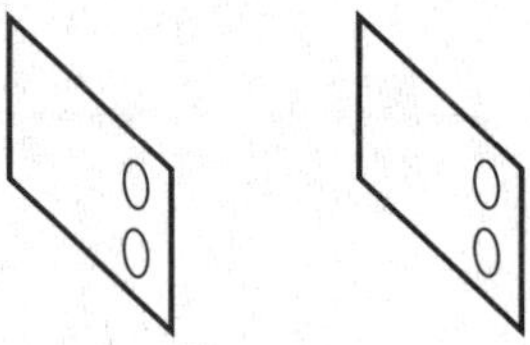

(SAME) **(OPPOSITE)**

Answer: SAME

4: Can the two flags be rotated into the same position?

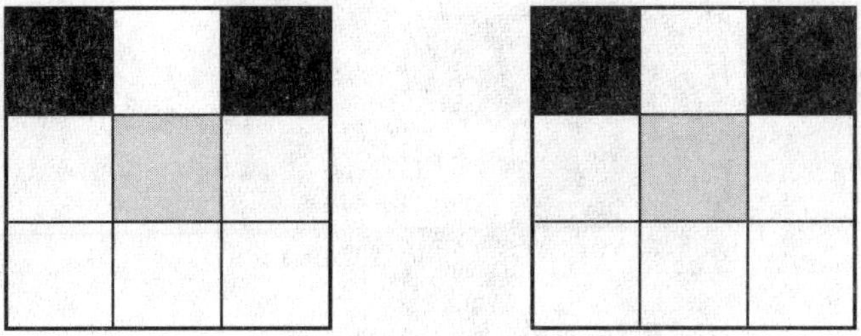

(YES) **(NO)**

Answer: YES

5: The square has been split into two pieces. Draw the two pieces in the square to show how they fit.

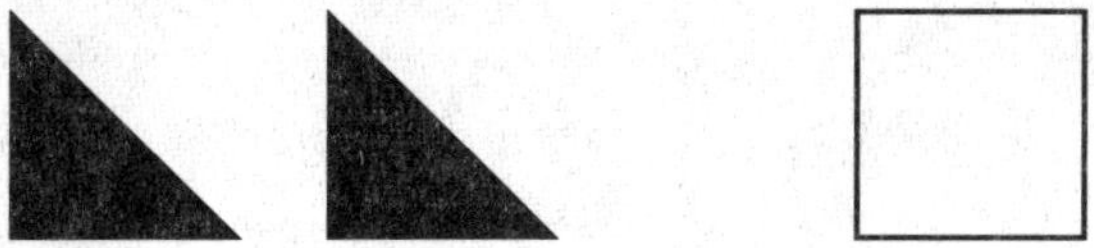

Answer: 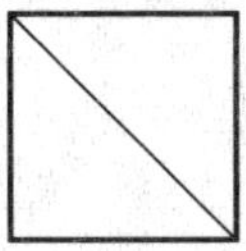

6: Which symbol is the odd one out?

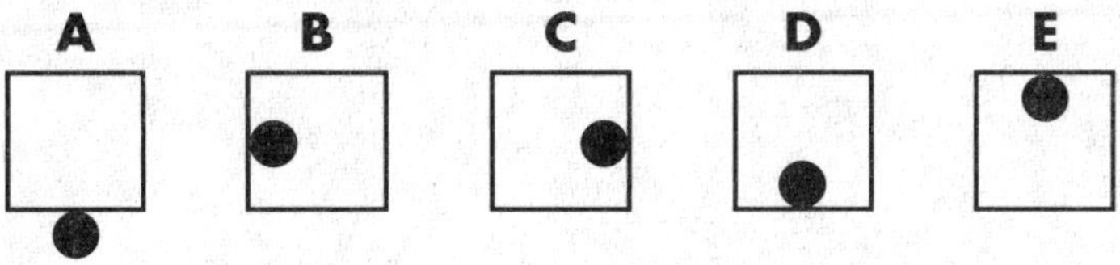

Answer: A

7: How many black squares are there? Write this number in the box.

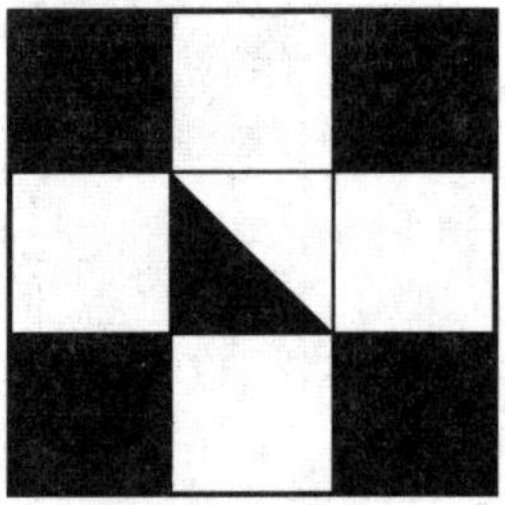

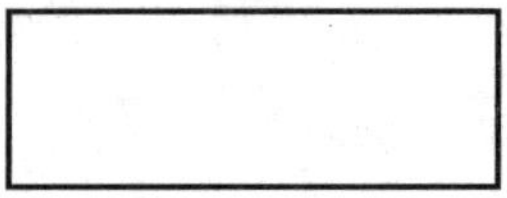

Answer: $4\frac{1}{2}$

Chapter 1

Tests for Children Aged 10–12

Abstract Reasoning

Insert the next number in the bracket.

1:	3	6	9	12	15	( )
2:	2	4	8	16	32	( )
3:	52	48	44	40	36	( )
4:	14	32	50	68	86	( )
5:	6	10	5	9	4	( )
6:	12	24	6	12	3	( )

Insert the next letter in the bracket.

A	B	C	D	E	F	G	H	I	J	K	L	M
1	2	3	4	5	6	7	8	9	10	11	12	13

N	O	P	Q	R	S	T	U	V	W	X	Y	Z
14	15	16	17	18	19	20	21	22	23	24	25	26

7:	C	E	G	I	K	( )
8:	V	R	N	J	F	( )
9:	A	F	K	P	U	( )
10:	J	L	I	K	H	( )
11:	F	G	I	L	P	( )
12:	A	B	D	H		( )

Underline whether the last sentence is TRUE or FALSE.

13: All dragons are carrots and all clocks are submarines. All carrots are clocks. Therefore all dragons are submarines.

(TRUE) (FALSE)

14: All bananas have twelve feet but some goats play the piano. All goats have twelve feet. Therefore all bananas can play the piano.

(TRUE) (FALSE)

15: All basketball players are mice and all flowers have six noses. Some basketball players have six noses. Therefore some mice are flowers.

(TRUE) (FALSE)

16: All slippers are airports and some apples have purple hair. All apples are airports. Therefore all slippers have purple hair.

(TRUE) (FALSE)

17: All socks like cooking and some chairs like mountain climbing. All chairs like cooking. Therefore some socks like mountain climbing.

(TRUE) (FALSE)

18: Jessica is older than Brian. Brian is older than Susan. Therefore Susan is older than Jessica.

(TRUE) (FALSE)

19: Philip is taller than Amy. Fred is smaller than Amy. Therefore Philip is taller than Fred.

(TRUE) (FALSE)

20: Graham is faster than Emily. Emily is faster than Tony. Therefore Tony is slower than Graham.

(TRUE) (FALSE)

21: Melissa is younger than Chris. Garth is older than Chris. Therefore Melissa is older than Garth.

(TRUE) **(FALSE)**

22: Roger is taller than Madeleine. Roger is smaller than Stan. Therefore Stan is smaller than Madeleine.

(TRUE) **(FALSE)**

23: Amanda is smaller than Sarah. Steve is taller than Ian. Rachel is smaller than Sarah. Sarah is smaller than Ian. Therefore Rachel is smaller than Ian.

(TRUE) **(FALSE)**

In the following, there is a rule which makes 'A' become 'B'. Underline which symbol 'C' will become if it follows the same rule.

24: **A B C 1 2 3 4 5**

25: **A B C 1 2 3 4 5**

26:

A	B	C		1	2	3	4	5
❑	⌗	❍		⌖	❑	❍	⌗	◆

27:

A	B	C		1	2	3	4	5
⊗	×	⊕		×	⊕	+	⊗	%

28:

A	B	C		1	2	3	4	5
∀	A	Ǝ		I	E	H	e	A

Insert the number of the missing symbol.

29:

♥	●	▲
●	▲	♥
▲	♥	( )

1	2	3	4
♥	●	✖	▲

30:

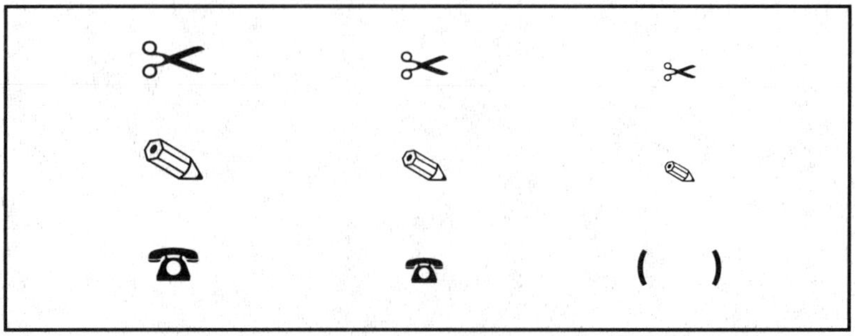

1	2	3	4

31:

)	O	(
/	|	\
>	=	( )

1	2	3	4
#	@	M	+

32:

1 2 3 4

33:

AE	QX	UB
WL	OG	IA
AZ	EI	( )

1	2	3	4
DL	IJ	AO	QU

34:

***	**	*
*	***	**
**	*	( )

1	2	3	4
*	**	***	****

35:

***	+ +	&
+	&&&	**
&&	*	( )

1	2	3	4	5
+ + +	***	+ +	&&	+

Insert the number of the next symbol in the series in box 'D'.

36: A B C D 1 2 3 4

37: A B C D 1 2 3 4

38: A B C D 1 2 3 4

39: A B C D 1 2 3 4

40: A B C D 1 2 3 4

Chapter 2

Tests for Children Aged 10–12

Numerical

Insert the numbers into the equation so that the equation is correct.

1: **3, 6, 8** _ + _ − _ = 11

2: **3, 4, 5** (_ x _) + _ = 19

3: **3, 4, 5, 8** (_ + _) − (_ + _) = 2

4: **4, 5, 7, 8** (_ x _) + (_ x _) = 68

5: **2, 3, 5, 7** (_ + _) / (_ x _) = 2

What are the solutions to the questions?

6: Peter can put up 6 shelves in an hour. Paul can put up 8 shelves in an hour. If they worked at that rate for 6 hours how many shelves will have been put up in total?

( )

7: The first minute of a telephone call costs 35 pence and every minute after that costs 28 pence. If Fiona speaks to Sandra on the telephone for 5 minutes, how much will the call cost?

( )

8: Mary bakes 40 cakes to be eaten equally by 7 people. If Mary eats 5 of the cakes before sharing them out, how many cakes will each person get?

( )

9: Bill is trying to get from the 1st floor to the 11th floor of an office block. If he can climb one floor every 50 seconds, how long will it take him to reach the 11th floor?

( )

10: In a recent knockout competition there were 16 teams. If each plays one match per round and the loser is eliminated from the competition, how many matches will the winning team have to play?

( )

Insert the missing number.

11:

5	9	6
4	11	5
8	9	( )

12:

8	4	6
5	1	2
9	17	( )

13:

12	4	14
7	10	13
18	2	( )

14:

2	4	6
9	6	3
4	5	( )

15:

8	2	4	6
3	7	1	9
5	3	8	( )

Insert the missing number.

16:

8

( ) 11

26 14

23 17

20

17:

18

( ) 30

21 42

15 14

9

18:

256

( ) 128

4 64

8 32

16

19:

2

( ) 4

36 9

16 12

8

20:

6

( ) 3

48 12

12 6

24

Insert the missing number.

21:

5	1	3
[8]	[10]	[ ]
1 2	3 6	2 4

22:

4	5	2
[24]	[15]	[ ]
3 2	1 3	4 6

23:

5 7	9 6	6 4
[4]	[8]	[ ]
8	7	9

24:

8 4 [7] 5	6 2 [4] 1	4 1 [ ] 8

25:

2 5 [9] 1 1	4 2 [14] 5 3	8 7 [ ] 6 5

Fill in the spaces in the tables.

26:

Cinema Audiences

	Morning	Afternoon	Evening	Total
Adult	5	13	35	
Child	12		0	
Total		47		99

27:

Fruit Stock

	Apples	Grapes	Lemons	Melons	Total
Shelf 1	15	3	26		50
Shelf 2	9		6	14	
Total		34			110

28:

Car Sales

	Red	Green	Black	Silver	Total
Manual	42			81	
Auto		32		51	200
Total	47	51	120		350

29:

Zoo Animals

	Zebras	Horses	Lions	Bears	Total
Male	8			18	87
Female		20	36		85
Total	12		83	43	

30:

Ice-Cream Sales

	Cone	Tub	Scoop	Lolly	Total
Small	21		17	34	80
Medium	14		13		79
Large	28			11	60
Total		66	36	54	

Fill in the spaces to meet the totals given with each question.

31: All rows add up to 19.

8	2	5	1	
3		8	2	1
	3	2	8	5
5	8	1	3	

32: All rows, columns and the two long diagonals add up to 10.

1		3	
	4	1	2
4	3	2	
	1		3

33: All rows, columns and the two long diagonals add up to 23.

	7	8	
8		6	7
2		7	
	6		8

34: All rows, columns and the two long diagonals add up to 20.

3	5		6	2
4		5	3	
	3		4	5
6		2		3
5		3		4

35: All rows, columns and the two long diagonals add up to 38.

	8	1		9
1	9		16	
	16	4		8
4		9	8	
8				1

Using the numbers in the key below, follow the instructions with each question to construct as many combinations as possible. You must only use a number once in any combination. You are not allowed to reverse a combination, so if you have written (4 + 6), for example, (6 + 4) is not a valid answer.

1	2	3	4	5	6	7	8	9

36: ADD 2 numbers to get 15.

a.

b.

37: ADD 3 numbers to get 22.

a.

b.

38: ADD 3 numbers to get 18.

a.

b.

c.

d.

e.

f.

g.

39: MULTIPLY 2 numbers to get 12.

a.

b.

40: MULTIPLY 3 numbers to get 24.

a.

b.

c.

Chapter 3

Tests for Children Aged 10–12

Perceptual

Using the key below, underline the set of numbers which matches each set of symbols.

1	2	3	4	5	6	7	8	9
@	$	=	)	>	£	+	#	<

1:

	£	>	<	@
a.	6	5	1	9
b.	2	6	9	5
c.	6	5	9	1
d.	6	2	5	1

a b c d

2:

	>	<	>	@	=	)
a.	5	9	5	2	3	4
b.	5	9	5	1	3	4
c.	9	5	9	1	3	4
d.	5	9	5	2	4	3

a b c d

3:

	=	)	>	<	)	$	$	)
a.	3	4	5	9	4	2	2	4
b.	3	5	4	9	2	4	2	4
c.	3	4	5	9	4	2	4	2
d.	3	4	5	9	4	4	2	2

a b c d

1	2	3	4	5	6	7	8	9
@	$	=	)	>	£	+	#	<

4:

	#	$	£	<	<	+	>	<	#	=
a.	8	2	6	9	9	7	9	5	8	3
b.	8	6	2	9	9	7	5	9	8	3
c.	8	2	6	9	9	7	9	5	8	3
d.	8	2	6	9	9	7	5	9	8	3

a b c d

5:

	+	<	>	#	#	)	=	>	<	>	)	@
a.	7	9	5	8	8	4	3	5	9	5	4	1
b.	7	5	5	8	8	3	4	9	5	5	4	1
c.	7	9	5	8	8	3	4	9	5	4	1	5
d.	7	5	9	8	8	4	3	5	9	5	4	1

a b c d

Each set of symbols in the code column represents a word in the word line. The same symbol represents the same letter in each question. In the translation column, write the words represented by each code.

6: words: MAT, TOP, RAM

code	**translation**
@ = #	
# = +	
+ $ >	

7: words: MOOSE, EXIST, BOOTS, STORE

code	**translation**
$ £ £ < #	
) £ £ = <	
< = £ & #	
# + ! < =	

8: words: SHAMED, HAMPER, SHRIMP, EXPORT

code	**translation**
= < £ ! (+	
$ = + # £ !	
(> !] + &	
$ = < £ ([	

9: words: BRACE, CAPER, CREEP, TRAIN, STEAL

code	translation
@ £ = + %	
$ [= = <	
£ [+ ! *	
$ + < = [	
> [+ $ =	

Underline whether the two words are spelt the SAME or DIFFERENTLY.

10:

SUSCEPTIBLENESS SUSCEPTABLENESS

(SAME) **(DIFFERENTLY)**

11:

CONGRATULATIONS CONGRATULATIONS

(SAME) **(DIFFERENTLY)**

12:

UNCOMPLIMENTARY UNCOMPLIMENTARY

(SAME) **(DIFFERENTLY)**

13:

MINIATURIZATION | MINITURIZATION

(SAME) **(DIFFERENTLY)**

14:

PHOTOSYNTHESIS | PHOTOSYNTHESIS

(SAME) **(DIFFERENTLY)**

15:

AMBIDEXTROUS | AMBIDEXTEROUS

(SAME) **(DIFFERENTLY)**

Underline whether the two numbers in each question are exactly the SAME or DIFFERENT.

16:

128968872146612954 | 128968872146112954

(SAME) **(DIFFERENT)**

17:

12112112213636363121 | 12112112213636363121

(SAME) **(DIFFERENT)**

18:

656566655656665612129 | 656566655656665612129

(SAME) **(DIFFERENT)**

19:

12345654321223456789 | 12345654321233456789

(SAME) **(DIFFERENT)**

20:

5676567656765671 23321	5676567656765671 23321
(SAME)	**(DIFFERENT)**

21:

23563265356226531919	23563265356226253191 9
(SAME)	**(DIFFERENT)**

In the key below a symbol stands for each number. Swop the numbers for the symbols to solve the equation in each question.

0	1	2	3	4	5	6	7	8	9
Z	Y	X	W	V	U	T	S	R	Q

22: **SX + YU – XZ** = ( )

23: **(YT ÷ V) + TWS** = ( )

24: **YUZ – SU + TR** = ( )

25: **TWS + YUR – YQX** = ( )

26: **YYUR – UZZ + YUZZ** = ( )

Which of the four numbered symbols is the same as the symbol on the left?

27: 1 2 3 4

(   )

28: 1 2 3 4

(   )

29: 1 2 3 4

(   )

30: 1 2 3 4

(   )

31: 1 2 3 4

★ ◆ ★ ✠ ▶

( )

Underline all consonants followed by a vowel and all vowels followed by a consonant.

32: O I H I R H I U F G F E W R Y A Z K A

33: I O D V H J V T V D V H D F A R X U I

34: Q W E U H W H D E V M A I A E P L E

35: A E I O U Z X T Y Q W U N O X A A S

36: V G H S D R Y T O U J H G D E D S F T

Underline all even numbers followed by an odd number and all odd numbers followed by an even number.

37: 3 5 7 5 5 5 7 8 9 6 6 3 2 4 3 5 7 8 9 8 5 4 3 5

38: 2 4 6 8 1 3 5 7 9 1 2 4 5 7 8 1 7 3 5 0 0 1 2 3

39: 1 8 7 5 4 5 4 3 5 7 9 9 4 3 6 5 7 8 7 6 5 5 9 2

40: 1 3 5 2 3 2 4 6 8 1 2 3 5 7 9 1 2 4 3 5 7 9 1 0

Chapter 4

Tests for Children Aged 10–12

Verbal

Underline whether the following words have the SAME or a DIFFERENT meaning.

1:

ABANDON	DESERT
(SAME)	**(DIFFERENT)**

2:

DECLINE	ACCEPT
(SAME)	**(DIFFERENT)**

3:

JUBILANT	MISERABLE
(SAME)	**(DIFFERENT)**

4:

CONFUSION	MAYHEM
(SAME)	**(DIFFERENT)**

5:

RELUCTANT	WILLING
(SAME)	**(DIFFERENT)**

6:

VARIATION	DIVERSITY
(SAME)	**(DIFFERENT)**

Fill in the missing letters so the words mean the same as the definition.

7:	A young cat.	**KI_T_N**
8:	To utter indistinctly.	**MU_B_E**
9:	Great fear, panic or dread.	**TE_R_R**
10:	A usual or habitual practice.	**CU_T_M**
11:	To regard with esteem	**AD_I_E**

Which two phrases are the closest in meaning?

12:
a. If at first you don't succeed, try, try again.
b. First come, first served.
c. Never give up despite disappointments.
d. Once bitten twice shy.

_ **and** _

13:
a. Turn the tables.
b. Foot the bill.
c. Take a short cut.
d. Put the shoe on the other foot.

_ **and** _

14:
a. Time and tide wait for no man.
b. Take one step at a time.
c. A bridge too far.
d. Don't cross the bridge until you come to it.

_ **and** _

15: **a.** **Have your fair share.**

b. **Best thing since sliced bread.**

c. **Food for thought.**

d. **Something to think about.**

_ and _

16: **a.** **Take your time.**

b. **Have your cake and eat it.**

c. **Burn the candle at both ends.**

d. **Look before you leap.**

_ and _

Each item in column (c) belongs either to column (a) or column (b). Underline which belongs to (a) and which belongs to (b).

17:

a	b	c		
CIRCLE	HOCKEY	DIAMOND	a	b
SQUARE	TENNIS	RECTANGLE	a	b
OBLONG	NETBALL	SQUASH	a	b
		RUGBY	a	b
		TRIANGLE	a	b

18:

a	b	c		
RED	SHEEP	COW	a	b
GREEN	HORSE	ORANGE	a	b
BROWN	CAT	DONKEY	a	b
		MOUSE	a	b
		BLUE	a	b

19:

a	b	c		
STOOL	BOAT	COUCH	a	b
CHAIR	CAR	FERRY	a	b
SETTEE	TRAIN	BENCH	a	b
		LORRY	a	b
		TRACTOR	a	b

20:

a	b	c		
CHEESE	PENCIL	CRAYON	a	b
BANANA	BIRO	MELON	a	b
TOAST	CHALK	CAKE	a	b
		PEN	a	b
		APPLE	a	b

21:

a	b	c		
THREE	TWO	EIGHT	a	b
NINE	TEN	SIX	a	b
ONE	FOUR	FIVE	a	b
		ELEVEN	a	b
		SEVEN	a	b

Underline the odd one out.

22:

a. FROG
b. JUMPER
c. SWEATER
d. PULLOVER

a b c d

23:

a. SHOE
b. SHIRT
c. BOOT
d. SANDAL

a b c d

24:

a. START
b. COMMENCE
c. BEGIN
d. CONCLUDE

a b c d

25:

a. ARRIVE
b. EXIT
c. DEPART
d. LEAVE

a b c d

Insert the words from the following anagrams.

26: NOMO ( )

27: AIFRY ( )

28: SOMEU ( )

29: OYWELL ( )

30: MINKDOG ( )

Underline whether the following jumbled sentences are TRUE or FALSE.

31: BARK SOME CATS

(TRUE) **(FALSE)**

32: HAS BRANCHES TREE A

(TRUE) **(FALSE)**

33: FOR ARE LISTENING EARS

(TRUE) **(FALSE)**

34: ON ARE CHAIRS SITTING FOR

(TRUE) **(FALSE)**

35: OF CAPITAL FRANCE THE IS LONDON

(TRUE) **(FALSE)**

36: HAS WHEELS BICYCLE SQUARE A

(TRUE) **(FALSE)**

Make as many words as you can from the following words (3 letters or over).

37: **CRIME**

a. e.
b. f.
c. g.
d. h.

38: **CROWN**

a. g.
b. h.
c. i.
d. j.
e. k.
f. l.

39: **TRICKY**

a. f.
b. g.
c. h.
d. i.
e. j.

40: **FLOAT**

a. g.
b. h.
c. i.
d. j.
e. k.
f. l.
m.

Chapter 5

Tests for Children Aged 10–12

Visuo-spatial

All blocks below are the same size and shape. Decide how many other blocks each block is touching and write this number in the table. Faces or sides touching count but corners do not.

1:

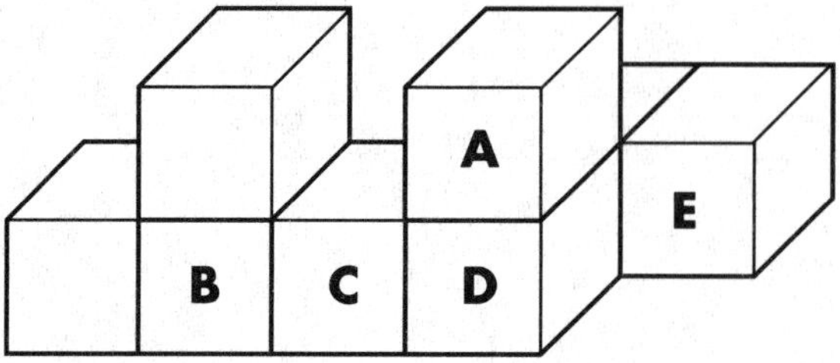

A	
B	
C	
D	
E	

2:

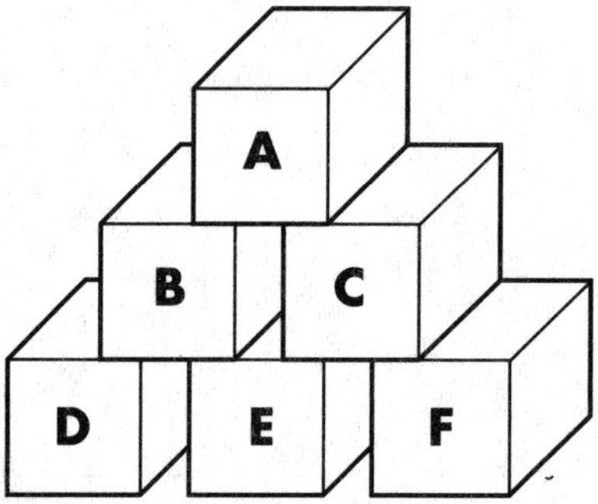

A	
B	
C	
D	
E	
F	

3:

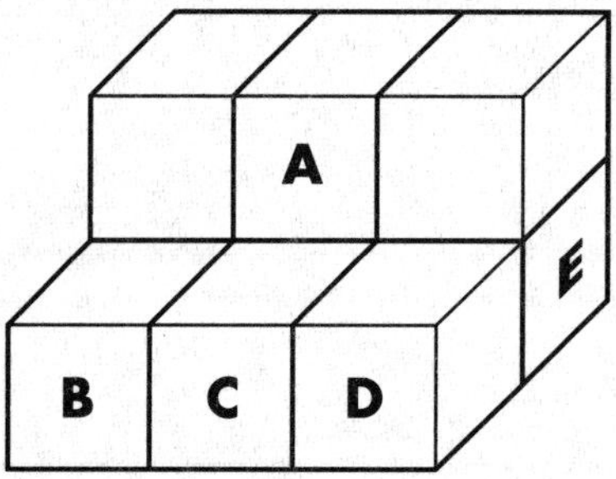

A	
B	
C	
D	
E	

4:

A	
B	
C	
D	
E	

5:

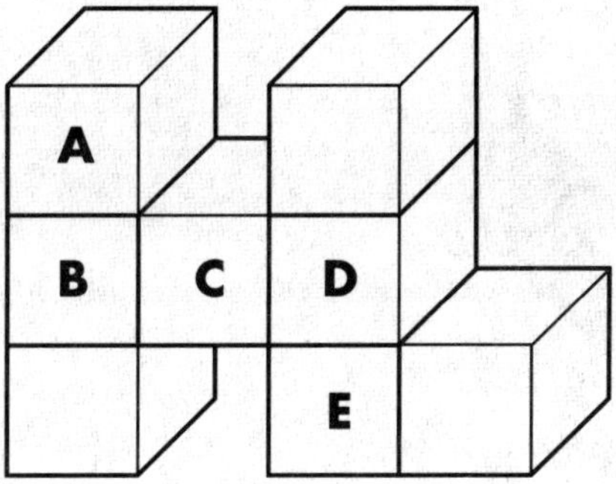

A	
B	
C	
D	
E	

6:

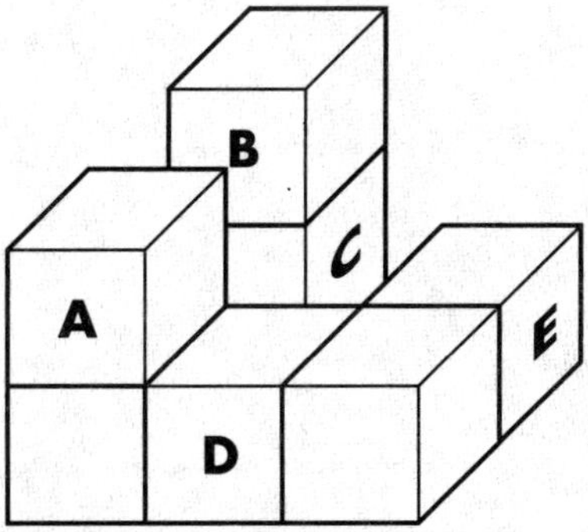

A	
B	
C	
D	
E	

Each side of the following cubes has a different design. If the two cubes are rotated, underline whether they will be the SAME or DIFFERENT.

7:

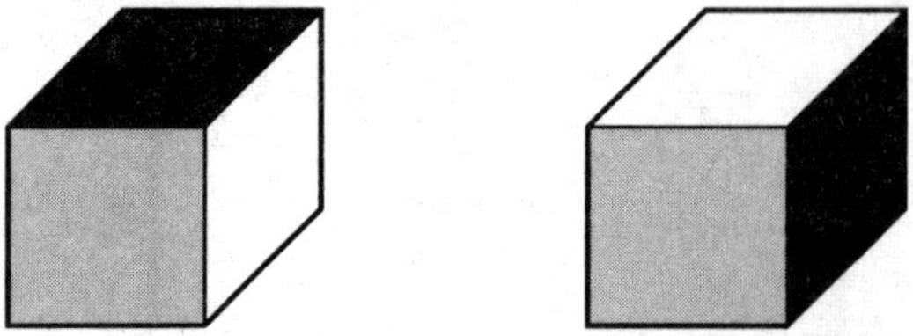

(SAME) **(DIFFERENT)**

8:

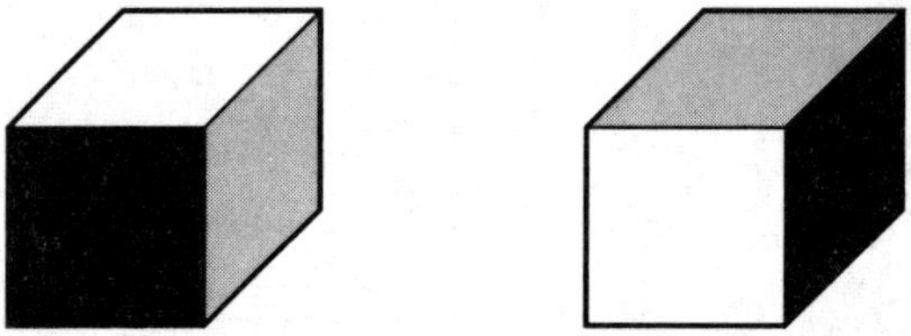

(SAME) **(DIFFERENT)**

9:

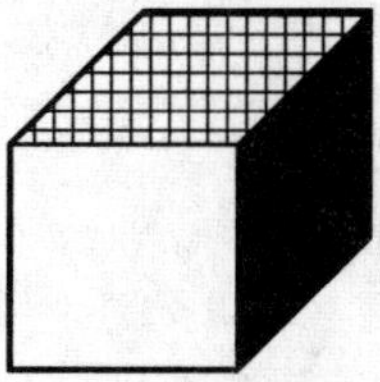

(SAME)

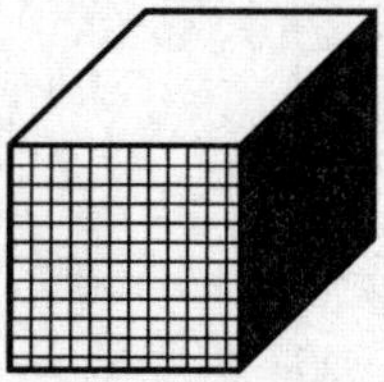

(DIFFERENT)

10:

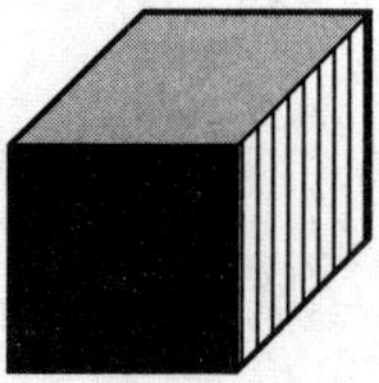

(SAME)

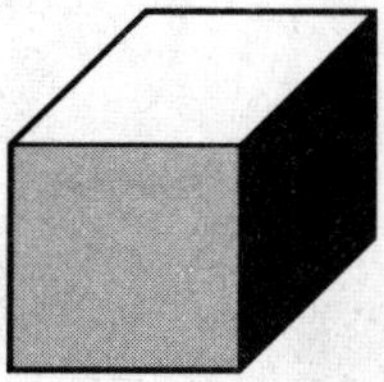

(DIFFERENT)

11:

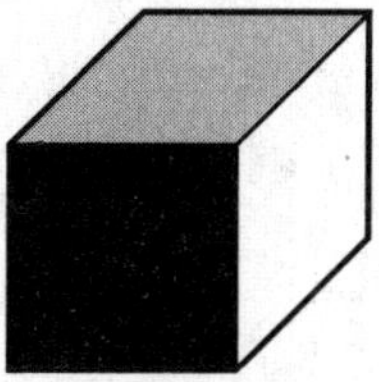

(SAME)

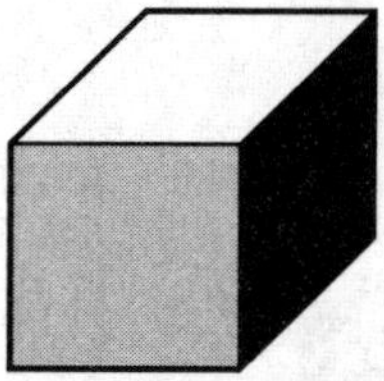

(DIFFERENT)

12:

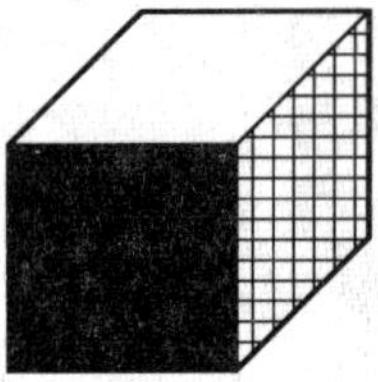

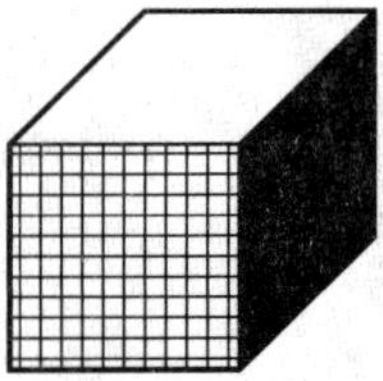

(SAME) **(DIFFERENT)**

Underline whether the two flags can be rotated into the same position.

13:

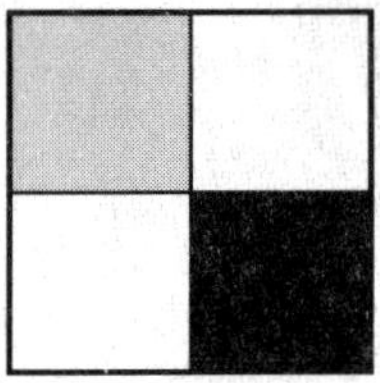

(YES) **(NO)**

14:

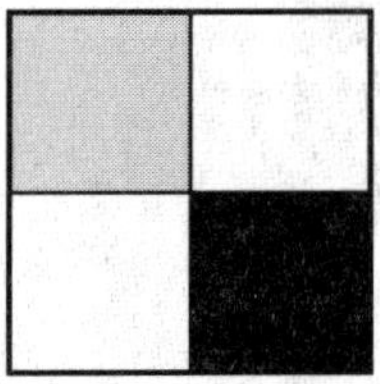

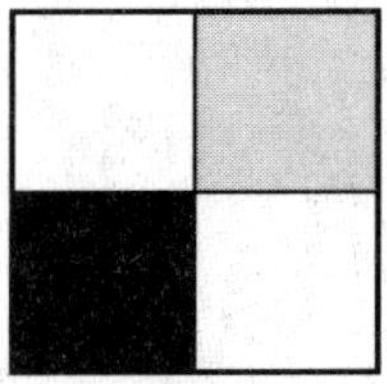

(YES) **(NO)**

15:

(YES)

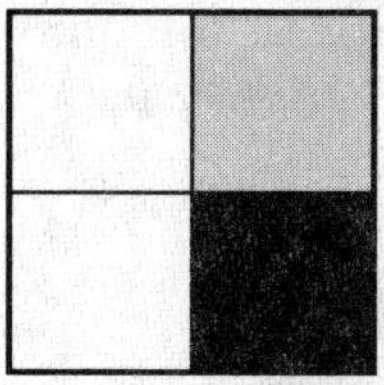

(NO)

16:

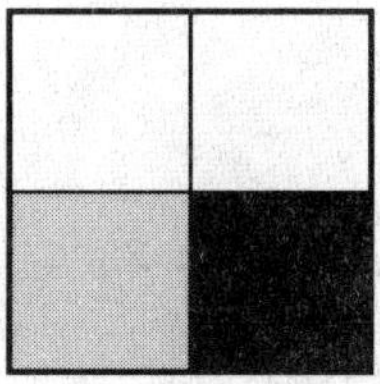

(YES)

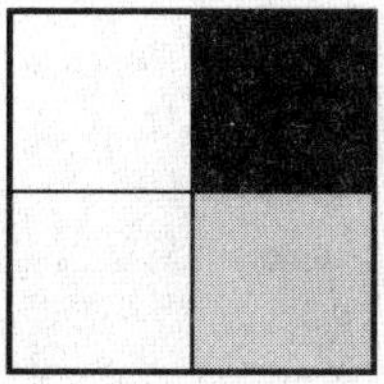

(NO)

17:

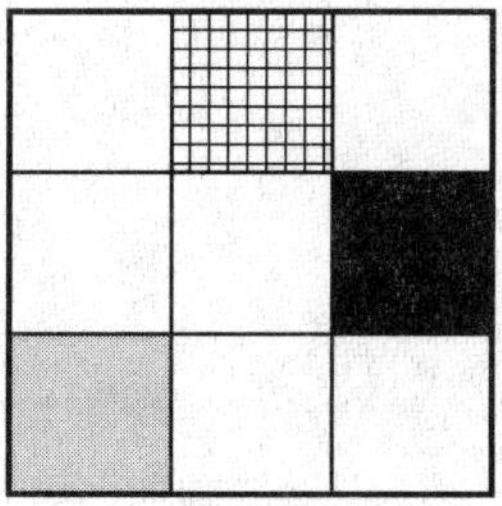

(YES)

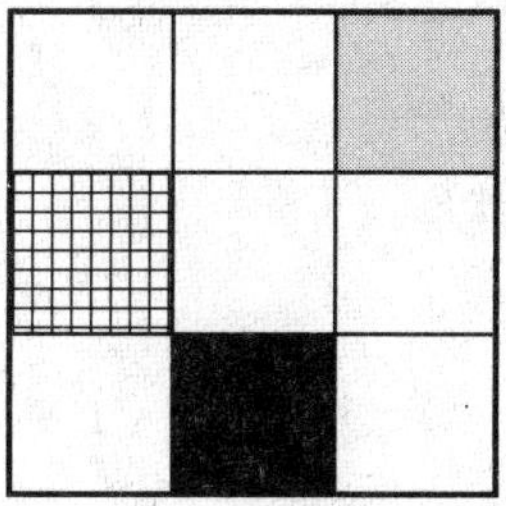

(NO)

18:

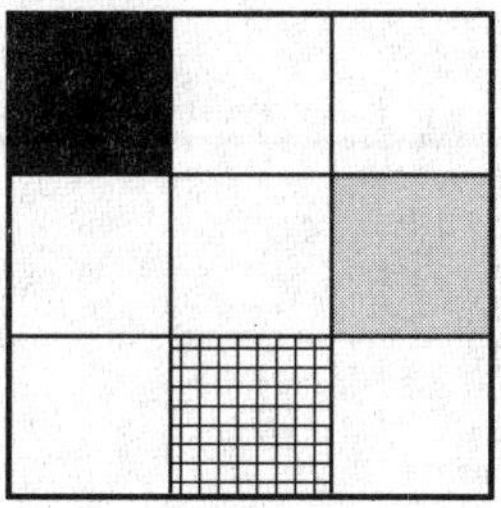

(YES)

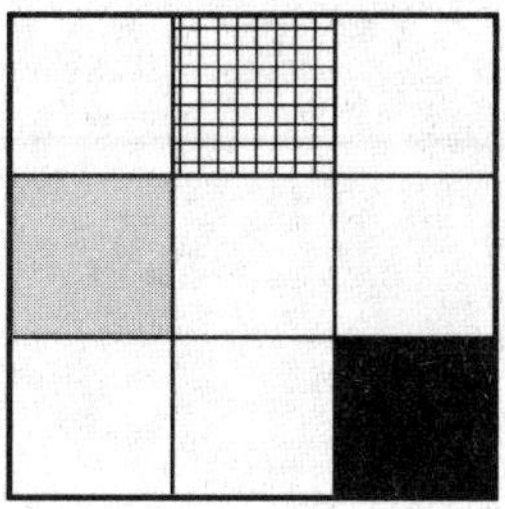

(NO)

The following shapes have been split into several pieces. Draw the pieces in the whole shape to show how they fit.

19:

20:

21:

22:

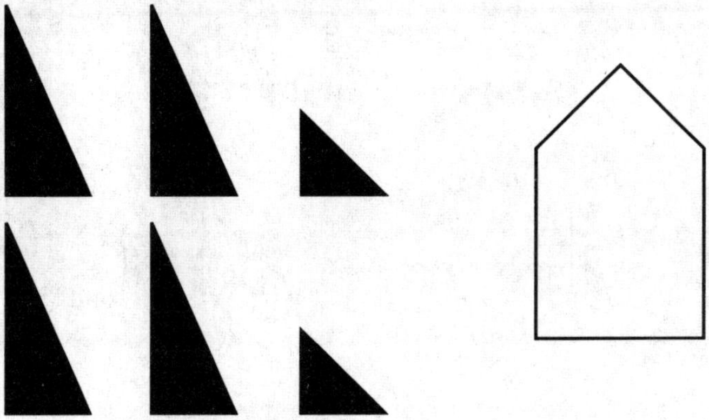

23:

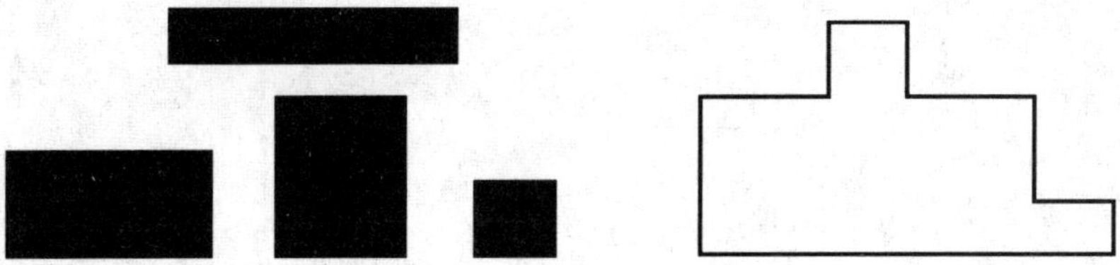

24:

Underline whether the two diagrams show the SAME side of the card or the OPPOSITE side.

25:

(SAME) **(OPPOSITE)**

26:

(SAME) **(OPPOSITE)**

27:

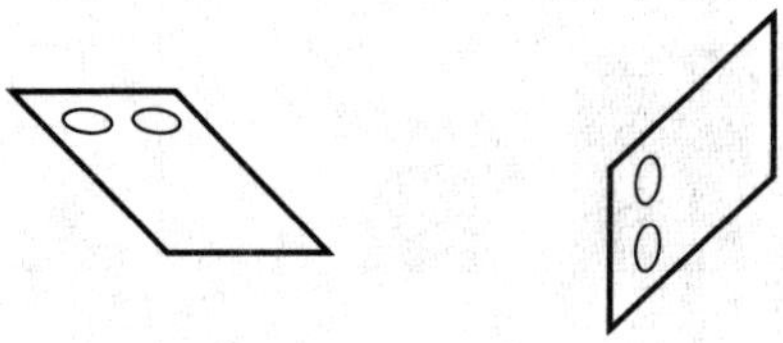

(SAME) **(OPPOSITE)**

28:

(SAME)

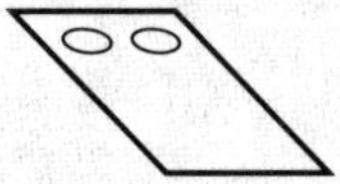

(OPPOSITE)

29:

(SAME)

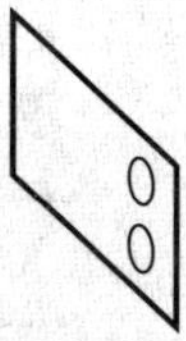

(OPPOSITE)

30:

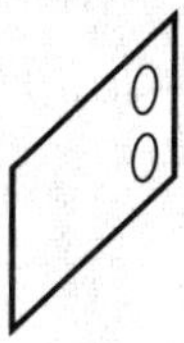

(SAME)

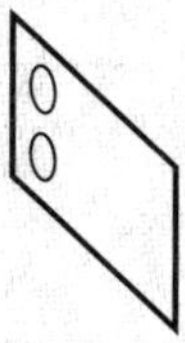

(OPPOSITE)

Underline the odd symbol out.

31: A B C D E

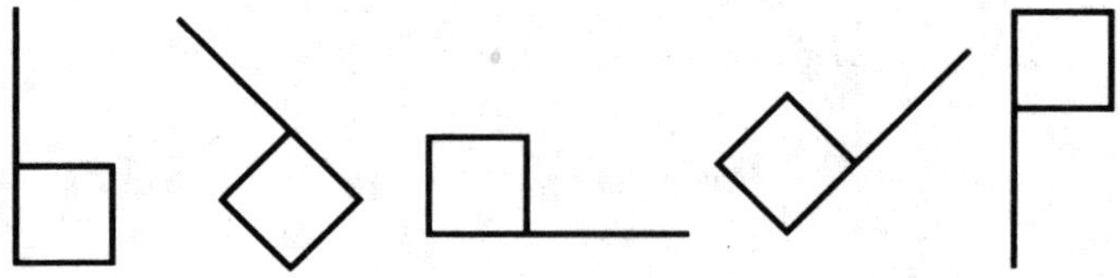

32: A B C D E

33: A B C D E

34: A B C D E

35: A B C D E

How many black squares are there? Write this number in the box.

36:

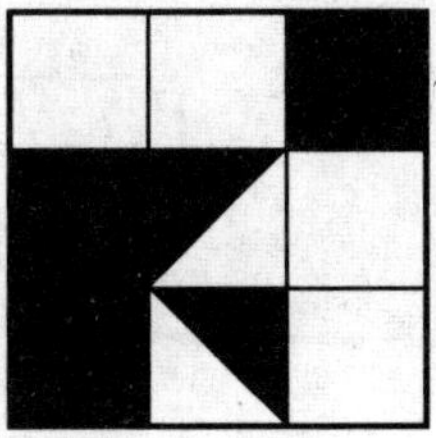

37:

38:

39:

40:

Chapter 6

Test Scoring System for Children Aged 10–12

Chapter 1

Questions 1–40:	2 points for each totally correct answer

Chapter 2

Questions 1–5:	1 point for each totally correct answer
Questions 6–25:	2 points for each totally correct answer
Questions 26–35:	per question: 4 parts correct = 1 point, 5 = 2, 7 = 3, 9 = 5
Questions 36–40:	per question: 2 parts correct = 1 point, 3 = 2, 7 = 3

Chapter 3

Questions 1–5:	1 point for each totally correct answer
Questions 6–31:	2 points for each totally correct answer
Questions 32–36:	per question: 4 parts correct = 1 point, 7 = 2, 10 = 3
Questions 37–40:	per question: 4 parts correct = 1 point, 7 = 2, 9 = 3, 12 = 4

Chapter 4

Questions 1–36:	1 point for each totally correct answer
Questions 37–40:	per question: 1 point for each correct word

Chapter 5

Question 1:	3 parts correct = 1 point, 5 = 2
Question 2:	3 parts correct = 1 point, 6 = 2
Questions 3–6:	per question: 3 parts correct = 1 point, 5 = 2
Questions 7–40:	2 points for each totally correct answer

Abstract Reasoning

1: **18**

2: **64**

3: **32**

4: **104**

5: **8**

6: **6**

7: **M**

8: **B**

9: **Z**

10: **J**

11: **U**

12: **P**

13: **TRUE**

14: **FALSE**

15: **FALSE**

16: **FALSE**

17: **FALSE**

18: **FALSE**

19: **TRUE**

20: **TRUE**

21: **FALSE**

22: **FALSE**

23: **TRUE**

24: **4**

25: **2**

26: **1**

27: **3**

28: **2**

29: **2**

30: **1**

31: **4**

32: **3**

33: **1**

34: **3**

35: **1**

36: **2**

37: **4**

38: **1**

39: **3**

40: **2**

Numerical

1: **6 + 8 − 3 = 11**

2: **(3 x 5) + 4 = 19**

3: **(3 + 8) − (4 + 5) = 2**

4: **(4 x 7) + (5 x 8) = 68**

5: **(5 + 7) / (2 x 3) = 2**

6: **84**

7: **£1.47**

8: **5**

9: **500 seconds or 8 minutes and 20 seconds**

10: **4**

11: **3**

12: **14**

13: **10**

14: **6**

15: **4**

16: **29**

17: **7**

18: **2**

19: **48**

20: **24**

21: **9**

22: **48**

23: **1**

24: **12**

25: **26**

26:

Cinema Audiences

	Morning	Afternoon	Evening	Total
Adult	5	13	35	53
Child	12	34	0	46
Total	17	47	35	99

27:

Fruit Stock

	Apples	Grapes	Lemons	Melons	Total
Shelf 1	15	3	26	6	50
Shelf 2	9	31	6	14	60
Total	24	34	32	20	110

28:

Car Sales

	Red	Green	Black	Silver	Total
Manual	42	19	8	81	150
Auto	5	32	112	51	200
Total	47	51	120	132	350

29:

Zoo Animals

	Zebras	Horses	Lions	Bears	Total
Male	8	14	47	18	87
Female	4	20	36	25	85
Total	12	34	83	43	172

30:

Ice-Cream Sales

	Cone	Tub	Scoop	Lolly	Total
Small	21	8	17	34	80
Medium	14	43	13	9	79
Large	28	15	6	11	60
Total	63	66	36	54	219

31: All rows add up to 19.

8	2	5	1	3
3	5	8	2	1
1	3	2	8	5
5	8	1	3	2

32: All rows, columns and the two long diagonals add up to 10.

1	2	3	4
3	4	1	2
4	3	2	1
2	1	4	3

33: All rows, columns and the two long diagonals add up to 23.

6	7	8	2
8	2	6	7
2	8	7	6
7	6	2	8

34: All rows, columns and the two long diagonals add up to 20.

3	5	4	6	2
4	2	5	3	6
2	3	6	4	5
6	4	2	5	3
5	6	3	2	4

35: All rows, columns and the two long diagonals add up to 38.

16	8	1	4	9
1	9	8	16	4
9	16	4	1	8
4	1	9	8	16
8	4	16	9	1

36:

a. $8 + 7$
b. $9 + 6$

37:

a. $9 + 8 + 5$
b. $9 + 7 + 6$

38:

a. $9 + 8 + 1$
b. $9 + 7 + 2$
c. $9 + 6 + 3$
d. $9 + 5 + 4$
e. $8 + 7 + 3$
f. $8 + 6 + 4$
g. $7 + 6 + 5$

39:

a. 2×6
b. 3×4

40:

a. $2 \times 3 \times 4$
b. $1 \times 4 \times 6$
c. $1 \times 3 \times 8$

Perceptual

1: c

2: b

3: a

4: d

5: a

6:

code	translation
@ = #	RAM
# = +	MAT
+ $ >	TOP

7:

code	translation
$ £ £ < #	MOOSE
) £ £ = <	BOOTS
< = £ & #	STORE
# + ! < =	EXIST

8:

code	translation
= < £ ! (+	HAMPER
$ = + # £ !	SHRIMP
(> !] + &	EXPORT
$ = < £ ([	SHAMED

9:

code	translation
@ £ = + %	STEAL
$ [= = <	CREEP
£ [+ ! *	TRAIN
$ + < = [	CAPER
> [+ $ =	BRACE

10: **DIFFERENT**

11: **SAME**

12: **SAME**

13: **DIFFERENT**

14: **SAME**

15: **DIFFERENT**

16: **DIFFERENT**

17: **SAME**

18: **SAME**

19: **DIFFERENT**

20: **SAME**

21: **DIFFERENT**

22: **TS or 67**

23: **TVY or 641**

24: **YVW or 143**

25: **TZW or 603**

26: **XYUR or 2158**

27: **3**

28: **2**

29: **1**

30: **4**

31: **2**

32: O **I** **H** **I** R **H** I **U** F G **F** **E** W R **Y** **A** Z **K** A

33: I **O** D V H J V T V D V H D **F** **A** R **X** U I

34: Q **W** E **U** H W H **D** **E** V **M** A I A **E** P **L** E

35: A E I O **U** Z X T Y Q **W** **U** **N** **O** **X** A **A** S

36: V G H S D R Y **T** O **U** J H G **D** **E** D S F T

37: 3 5 7 5 5 5 **7** **8** **9** 6 **6** **3** 2 **4** 3 5 **7** **8** **9** **8** **5** **4** 3 5

38: 2 4 6 **8** 1 3 5 7 9 **1** 2 **4** 5 **7** **8** 1 7 3 **5** 0 **0** **1** **2** 3

39: **1** **8** 7 **5** **4** **5** **4** 3 5 7 9 **9** **4** **3** **6** 5 **7** **8** **7** **6** 5 5 **9** 2

40: 1 3 **5** **2** **3** 2 4 6 **8** **1** **2** 3 5 7 9 **1** 2 **4** 3 5 7 9 **1** 0

Verbal

1: **Same**

2: **Different**

3: **Different**

4: **Same**

5: **Different**

6: **Same**

7: **Kitten**

8: **Mumble**

9: **Terror**

10: **Custom**

11: **Admire**

12: **a and c**

13: **a and d**

14: **b and d**

15: **c and d**

16: **a and d or b and c**

17:

Diamond	**a**
Rectangle	**a**
Squash	**b**
Rugby	**b**
Triangle	**a**

18:

Cow	**b**
Orange	**a**
Donkey	**b**
Mouse	**b**
Blue	**a**

19:

Couch	**a**
Ferry	**b**
Bench	**a**
Lorry	**b**
Tractor	**b**

20:

Crayon	**b**
Melon	**a**
Cake	**a**
Pen	**b**
Apple	**a**

21:

Eight	**b**
Six	**b**
Five	**a**
Eleven	**a**
Seven	**a**

22: **a**

23: **b**

24: **d**

25: **a**

26: **Moon**

27: **Fairy**

28: **Mouse**

29: **Yellow**

30: **Kingdom**

31: **False**

32: **True**

33: **True**

34: **True**

35: **False**

36: **False**

37:	RICE	RIM	RIME	
	ICE	IRE		
	MICE	MIRE	EMIR	
38:	CROW	CORN	COW	CON
	ROW	OWN	ORC	ROC
	WORN	WON	NOR	NOW
39:	TRICK	TRY	TIC	TICK
	RICK	IRK	ICY	
	CRY	CITY	KIT	
40:	FLAT	FOAL	FAT	ALT
	LOFT	LOAF	LOT	
	OFT	OAF	OAT	
	AFT	ALOFT	ALTO	

Visuo-spatial

1: A 3
B 3
C 5
D 4
E 2

2:
A 2
B 3
C 3
D 1
E 2
F 1

3:
A 6
B 4
C 6
D 4
E 4

4:
A 3
B 1
C 3
D 2
E 1

5:
A 2
B 3
C 6
D 4
E 2

6: **A 2**
B 1
C 1
D 4
E 2

7: **DIFFERENT**

8: **SAME**

9: **SAME**

10: **DIFFERENT**

11: **SAME**

12: **DIFFERENT**

13: **YES**

14: **YES**

15: **NO**

16: **YES**

17: **NO**

18: **YES**

19:

20:

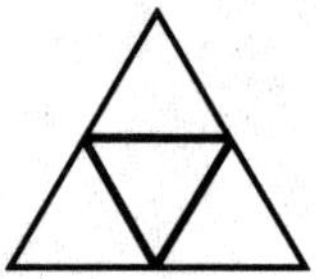

21:

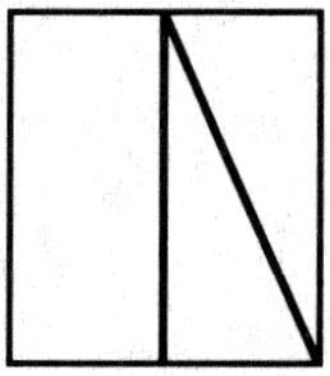

22:

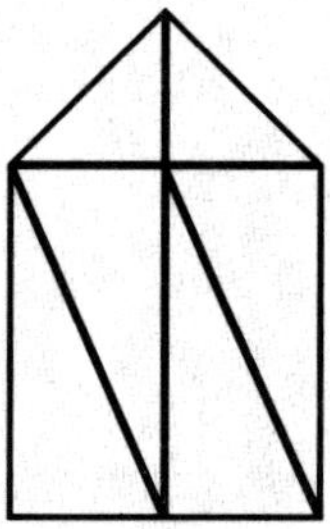

23:

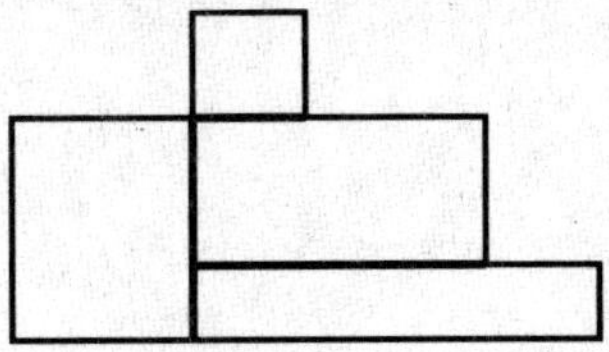

24:

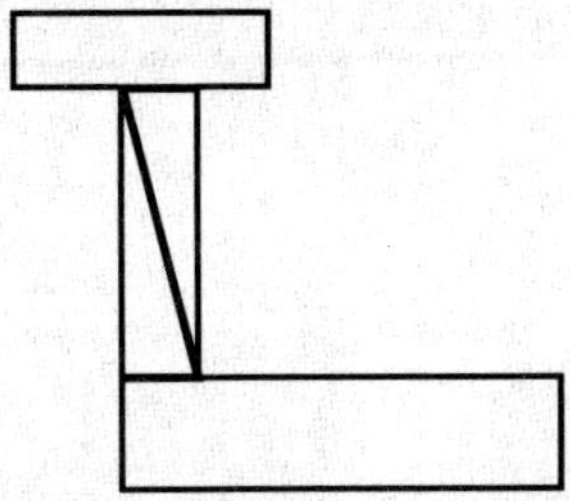

25: **SAME**

26: **OPPOSITE**

27: **SAME**

28: **OPPOSITE**

29: **SAME**

30: **OPPOSITE**

31: **A**

32: **D**

33: **C**

34: **D**

35: **C**

36: **4**

37: **6**

38: **6**

39: **8 $\frac{1}{2}$**

40: **10**

Profile of Abilities and IQ Conversion Tables

IQ and Profile of Abilities for Children Aged 10–12

The first step is to score each of the five ability tests. Having done that, look at the Test Score Table appropriate for your age, and see whether your score on each of the five tests is in the Outstanding, Excellent, Very Good, Good, Adequate or Fair category. Now look at the table below and put an X in the category you have achieved. The pattern of X marks is a profile of your abilities.

	Test 1 **Abstract Reasoning**	**Test 2** **Numerical**	**Test 3** **Perceptual**	**Test 4** **Verbal**	**Test 5** **Visuo-spatial**
1 Outstanding					
2 Excellent					
3 Very Good					
4 Good					
5 Adequate					
6 Fair					

Test Score Table for Children Aged 10

	Test 1 Abstract Reasoning	Test 2 Numerical	Test 3 Perceptual	Test 4 Verbal	Test 5 Visuo-spatial
1 Oustanding	Above 71	Above 57	Above 71	Above 47	Above 65
2 Excellent	68–71	50–57	67–71	44–47	60–65
3 Very Good	64–67	42–49	62–66	40–43	54–59
4 Good	60–63	34–41	57–61	36–39	48–53
5 Adequate	56–59	26–33	52–56	32–35	42–47
6 Fair	Below 56	Below 26	Below 52	Below 32	Below 42

Test Score Table for Children Aged 11

	Test 1 **Abstract Reasoning**	**Test 2** **Numerical**	**Test 3** **Perceptual**	**Test 4** **Verbal**	**Test 5** **Visuo-spatial**
1 Outstanding	Above 73	Above 61	Above 73	Above 51	Above 67
2 Excellent	70–73	54–61	69–73	48–51	62–67
3 Very Good	66–69	46–53	64–68	44–47	56–61
4 Good	62–65	38–45	59–63	40–43	50–55
5 Adequate	58–61	30–37	54–58	36–39	44–49
6 Fair	Below 58	Below 30	Below 54	Below 36	Below 44

Test Score Table for Children Aged 12

	Test 1 Abstract Reasoning	Test 2 Numerical	Test 3 Perceptual	Test 4 Verbal	Test 5 Visuo-spatial
1 Outstanding	Above 75	Above 65	Above 75	Above 55	Above 69
2 Excellent	72–75	58–65	71–75	52–55	64–69
3 Very Good	68–71	50–57	66–70	48–51	58–63
4 Good	64–67	42–49	61–65	44–47	52–57
5 Adequate	60–63	34–41	56–60	40–43	46–51
6 Fair	Below 60	Below 34	Below 56	Below 40	Below 46

IQ Conversion Table for Children
Aged 10–12 Years

To obtain your IQ, add together all five of your ability scores. Enter this total score at the bottom of the IQ Conversion Table below. Find the appropriate age level and read off the IQ corresponding to your score.

Score			Intelligence
Age 10	**Age 11**	**Age 12**	**IQ**
295	310	325	160
287	302	317	155
280	295	310	150
272	287	302	145
265	280	295	140
257	272	287	135
250	265	280	130
242	257	272	125
235	250	265	120
227	242	257	115
220	235	250	110
212	227	242	105
205	220	235	100
	Score:	**IQ:**	

Chapter 7

Tests for Children Aged 13–15

Abstract Reasoning

Insert the next number.

1:		37	45	53	61	( )
2:		152	134	116	98	( )
3:		3	9	27	81	( )
4:		85	91	76	82	( )
5:	10	32	16	38	19	( )
6:	14	24	36	46	69	( )

Insert the next letter.

A	B	C	D	E	F	G	H	I	J	K	L	M
1	2	3	4	5	6	7	8	9	10	11	12	13

N	O	P	Q	R	S	T	U	V	W	X	Y	Z
14	15	16	17	18	19	20	21	22	23	24	25	26

7:	C	G	K	O	S			( )
8:	V	S	P	M	J			( )
9:	H	M	F	K	D			( )
10:	B	D	E	J	K			( )
11:	X	L	P	H	L	F		( )
12:	B	D	C	E	D	F	( )	( )

In the following sentences, underline whether the final sentence is TRUE or FALSE.

13: **All pencils are cupboards and all telephones are pizzas. All cupboards are telephones. Therefore all cupboards are pizzas.**

(TRUE) (FALSE)

14: **All ducks have green beaks and some chairs can speak French. If all ducks speak French, then all chairs have green beaks.**

(TRUE) (FALSE)

15: **All parrots are sinks and some chess pieces are vegetarian. If all record players and parrots are vegetarian, then no sinks are vegetarian.**

(TRUE) (FALSE)

16: **All wheels are trees and all grapes have three feet. If some wheels play snooker and all wheels have three feet, then some grapes play snooker.**

(TRUE) (FALSE)

17: All dice can fly backwards but some cards can fly forwards. All bananas wear glasses. If all cards are dice and some bananas can fly backwards, then some dice wear glasses.

(TRUE) (FALSE)

18: Alfred is taller than Peter. Mary is smaller than Peter. Therefore Alfred is smaller than Mary.

(TRUE) (FALSE)

19: Florence is smaller than Gemma. Colin is taller than Susan. Florence is taller than Colin. Therefore Susan is taller than Florence.

(TRUE) (FALSE)

20: Michael is older than George. Amanda is younger than Sandra. Michael is the second oldest. Amanda is older than George. Therefore Sandra is the oldest.

(TRUE) (FALSE)

21: **Pam is older than Martin. David is younger than Martin and Toby. Sharon and Toby are older than Martin. Therefore David is older than Sharon.**

(TRUE) (FALSE)

22: **Polly is younger than Paul. Brian is younger than Sam. Sam is the oldest. Polly is older than Brian. Therefore Brian is the youngest.**

(TRUE) (FALSE)

23: **Rachel and Bruce are older than Harry. Harry is younger than Larry. Fiona is older than Bruce. Harry is older than Louise. Fiona is younger than Rachel. Therefore Rachel is older than Bruce and Larry is older than Louise.**

(TRUE) (FALSE)

In the following, there is a rule which makes 'A' become 'B'. Underline which symbol 'C' will become if it follows the same rule.

	A	B	C	1	2	3	4	5
24:	è	é	ù	ý	ù	ê	ú	û

	A	B	C	1	2	3	4	5
25:	●	○	◆	★	◇	□	⇒	Δ

	A	B	C	1	2	3	4	5
26:	═	≡	+	⊕	✚	±	≊	✦

	A	B	C	1	2	3	4	5
27:	⑧	❹	6					

	A	B	C	1	2	3	4	5
28:	10	X	100	L	M	I	D	C

Insert the number of the missing symbol.

29:

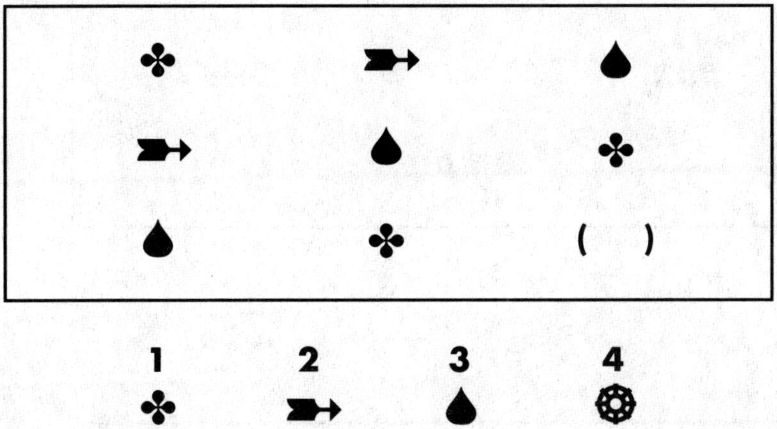

30:

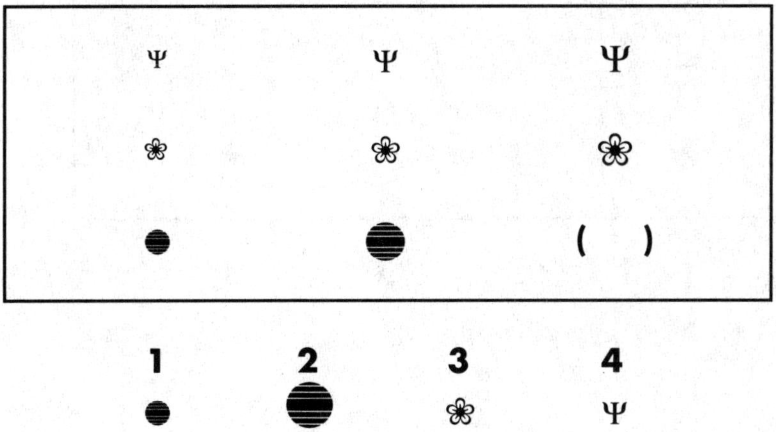

31:

**	+++	#
###	*	++
+	##	( )

1	2	3	4
***	**	+++	###

32:

1 2 3 4

33:

TV	UM	AE
OI	PK	IZ
AG	OO	( )

1	2	3	4
WF	EL	MI	IR

34:

***+	*++	**+++
*++	**+++	***+
**+++	***+	( )

1	2	3	4
*+++	**+	***++	*++

35:

#>>>@@	##>@@@	###>>@
##>@@@	###>>@	#>>>@@
###>>@	#>>>@@	( )

1	2	3
#>>@@@	##>>>@	##>@@
4	**5**	**6**
##>@@@	###>@@	##>@

Insert the number of the next symbol in the series in box 'D'.

36:

37:

38:

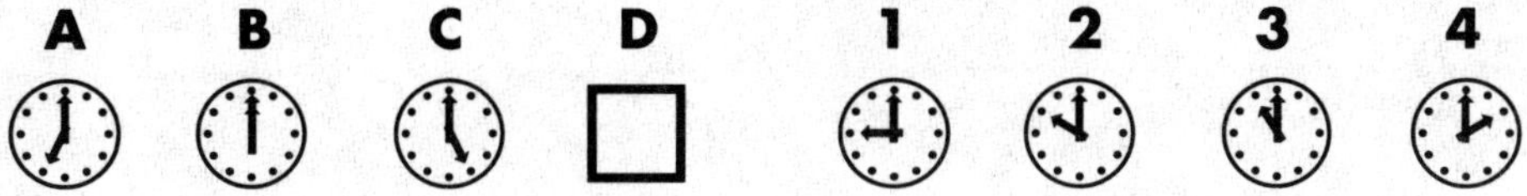

39:

40:

A	B	C	D	1	2	3	4
a	<g>	<m>		*u*	<s>	<u>	*s*

Chapter 8

Tests for Children Aged 13–15

Numerical

Insert the numbers into the equation so that the equation is correct.

1: **2, 4, 5, 8** **(_ + _) - (_ + _) = 5**

2: **3, 6, 7, 9** **(_ x _) + (_ - _) = 24**

3: **4, 5, 6, 7** **(_ + _) / (_ - _) = 5**

4: **2, 5, 6, 9** **(_ + _) x (_ / _) = 42**

5: **2, 4, 5, 8** **(_ x _) / (_ x _) = 5**

What are the solutions to these questions?

6: Martin can put up 24 shelves in 3 hours. Alan can put up 8 shelves in half an hour. If they worked at that rate for 6 hours how many shelves will have been put up in total?

( )

7: The first minute of a telephone call costs 42 pence and every minute after that costs 30 pence. If Alison speaks to Mary on the telephone for $14\frac{1}{2}$ minutes, how much will the call cost? (No rounding up.)

( )

8: Cathy bakes 95 cakes to be eaten equally by 12 people. If Cathy eats 11 of the cakes before sharing them out, how many cakes will each person get?

( )

9: Edward is trying to get from the 13th floor to the 42nd floor of an office block. If he can climb one floor every 58 seconds, how long will it take him to reach the 42nd floor?

( )

10: In a recent knockout competition there were 32 players. If each plays one match per round and the loser is eliminated from the competition, how many matches will the winning player have to play?

( )

Insert the missing number.

11:

8	**3**	**6**
6	**10**	**12**
7	**8**	**( )**

12:

5	14	16
19	4	12
9	15	( )

13:

10	4	8	9
7	6	5	13
14	6	8	3
5	20	2	( )

14:

8	4	36	12
20	12	4	6
14	8	6	18
8	26	4	( )

15:

12	16	18	10	4
8	36	2	12	2
25	16	8	3	8
10	12	31	4	3
5	16	3	6	( )

Insert the missing number.

16:

4

( ) 12

52 20

44 28

36

17:

4

( ) 8

256 16

128 32

64

18:

130

( ) 114

34 98

50 82

66

19:

8

( ) 3

24 12

6 9

16

20:

12

( ) 18

2 6

6 21

4

Insert the missing number.

21:

3	6	7
[16]	[15]	[ ]
9 4	5 4	9 1

22:

7	8	4
[42]	[32]	[ ]
2 3	4 1	3 6

23:

4 5	9 2	7 3
[3]	[5]	[ ]
6	6	5

24:

9 3	4 1	8 4
[7]	[9]	[ ]
4	5	3

25:

7 2	5 9	8 9
[18]	[21]	[ ]
4 5	6 1	4 6

Fill in the spaces in the tables.

26:

Cinema Audiences

	Morning	Afternoon	Evening	Total
Adult		86		
Child	52		100	300
Total	100		150	

27:

Ice-Cream Sales

	Cone	Tub	Scoop	Lolly	Total
Small	58		39	25	
Medium		25		48	221
Large	22			26	100
Total	166	85	103		

28:

Music Sales

	Jazz	Soul	Dance	Other	Total
Male		32	54		166
Female	46		32	38	150
Group	18		49	26	
Total		93		106	

29:

Tournament Entries

	U-10	U-14	U-18	Open	Total
Male	45	56	67	78	
Female		36			
Doubles	24	48	36	16	
Total	87		157		500

30:

Buffet Sales

	Tea	Coffee	Crisps	Nuts	Total
Small		89	59	36	
Medium	67		28		164
Large	43	123		95	
Total		270	133		758

Fill in the spaces to meet the totals given with each question.

31: All rows add up to 57.

	13	19	9	6
27	5	11		2
16		18	13	7
6	27		18	5

32: All rows, columns and the two long diagonals add up to 114.

12		34	
	45	12	23
45	34	23	
	12		34

33: All rows, columns and the two long diagonals add up to 123.

	17	28	
28		36	17
42		17	
	36		28

34: All rows, columns and the two long diagonals add up to 90.

23	25		16	12
14		25	23	
	23		14	25
16		12		23
25		23		14

35: All rows, columns and the two long diagonals add up to 178.

	38	41		49
41	49		16	
	16	34		38
34		49	38	
38				41

Using the numbers in the key below, follow the instructions with each question to construct as many combinations as possible. You must only use a number once in any combination. You are not allowed to reverse a combination, so if you have written (4 + 6), for example, (6 + 4) is not a valid answer.

1	2	3	4	5	6	7	8	9

36: ADD 2 numbers to get 12.

a.

b.

c.

37: ADD 3 numbers to get 19.

a.

b.

c.

d.

e.

38: MULTIPLY 3 numbers to get 30.

a.

b.

39: ADD 3 numbers to get 15.

a.

b.

c.

d.

e.

f.

g.

h.

40: MULTIPLY 3 numbers to get 40.

a.

b.

Chapter 9

Tests for Children Aged 13–15

Perceptual

Using the key below, underline the set of numbers which matches each set of symbols.

1	2	3	4	5	6	7	8	9
%	#	=	$	<	@	!	)	>

1:

	#	)	$	%	=
a.	3	6	4	1	2
b.	6	8	4	2	3
c.	2	8	5	1	3
d.	2	8	4	1	3

a b c d

2:

	>	<	>	)	<	#
a.	5	9	5	8	9	2
b.	9	5	9	8	5	2
c.	9	5	9	8	2	5
d.	5	9	5	8	5	2

a b c d

3:

	=	>	%	!	#	>	$	>
a.	3	9	1	7	2	9	4	9
b.	3	5	1	7	2	5	6	9
c.	2	9	1	7	3	9	4	9
d.	3	9	7	1	3	4	9	4

a b c d

1	2	3	4	5	6	7	8	9
%	#	=	$	<	@	!	)	>

4:

	)	>	)	<	)	#	>	#	!	!	)	>
a.	7	9	8	5	8	2	9	2	7	7	9	8
b.	8	5	8	5	8	2	5	2	7	7	8	9
c.	7	5	8	5	8	2	5	2	7	7	8	9
d.	8	9	8	5	8	2	9	2	7	7	8	9

a   b   c   d

5:

	#	%	#	$	#	!	>	<	>	<	)	!	@
a.	2	1	2	4	2	7	5	9	5	9	8	7	6
b.	1	2	1	4	1	7	5	9	5	9	8	7	6
c.	2	1	2	4	2	7	9	5	9	5	8	7	6
d.	1	2	1	4	2	7	9	5	9	5	8	7	6
e.	2	1	2	4	2	7	9	5	9	5	6	7	8

a   b   c   d   e

Each set of symbols in the code column represents a word in the word line. The same symbol represents the same letter in each question. In the translation column, write the words represented by each code.

6: Words: CREEP, FLOAT, PIECE, CRAFT

code	**translation**
+) # & $	
& = > # $	
+) £ £ @	
@ [£ + £	

7: Words: BREEZE, AROUND, CARROT, BEFORE, DEPEND

code	**translation**
& £ (> + £	
$ = + + > <	
# £ ! £ @ #	
= + > %@ #	
& + £ £ * £	

8: Words: HONOUR, RADISH, MENACE, REMIND, FINISH

code	translation
< & (£ $ >	
% # $ # @ <	
< ! > £) %	
* £ $ £) %	
(& $! + &	

9: Words: TORRENT, RETIRES, SHATTER, PERFECT, SMITTEN, STRIPES

code	translation
* # $ ((£ >	
> £ (& > £ *	
(@ > > £ < (	
* + & ((£ <	
* (> & = £ *	
= £ > ~ £ [(	

10: Words: EXTRACT, APPEARS, COMPLEX, WRIGGLE, ERRATIC, TREMBLE

code	**translation**
+ (* % > < *	
@ (! $ $ < *	
* & + ( ) £ +	
) ~ ~ *) (=	
* (( ) + ! £	
£ # % ~ < * &	

Underline whether the two words in each question are spelt the SAME or DIFFERENTLY.

11:

MULTIMILLIONAIRE MULTIMILLIONNAIRE

(SAME) **(DIFFERENTLY)**

12:

HUMANITARIANISM HUMANITARIANISM

(SAME) **(DIFFERENTLY)**

13:

ONOMATOPOEICALLY ONOMATOPEICALLY

(SAME) **(DIFFERENTLY)**

14: DENDROCHRONOLOGY DENDROCHRONOLOGY

(SAME) **(DIFFERENTLY)**

15: MILLENARIANISM MILLENARIANISM

(SAME) **(DIFFERENTLY)**

16: SESQUICENTENNIAL SESQUISCENTENNIAL

(SAME) **(DIFFERENTLY)**

Underline which two numbers in each question are the SAME or DIFFERENT.

17:

123123211212121224141 123123211211212124141

(SAME) **(DIFFERENT)**

18:

18592301187620973252 18592301187620967325 2

(SAME) **(DIFFERENT)**

19:

5491045536758490 2019 5491045536758490 2019

(SAME) **(DIFFERENT)**

20:

39399393399313131393 39399399339313131393

(SAME) **(DIFFERENT)**

21:

12345432123454321234 12345432123454321234

(SAME) **(DIFFERENT)**

22:

23443322343234322223 234433223432343222223

(SAME) **(DIFFERENT)**

In the key below a letter stands for each number. Swop the numbers for the letters to solve the equation in each question.

0	1	2	3	4	5	6	7	8	9
T	S	R	Q	P	O	N	M	L	K

23: **RQP – ON + SRL** = ( )

24: **PO x QT** = ( )

25: **LSRP + QTOP – RNLO** = ( )

26: **KT ÷ PO** = ( )

27: **NTOP – QKKT + PNTN** = ( )

Which of the four numbered symbols is the same as the symbol on the left?

28: **1 2 3 4**

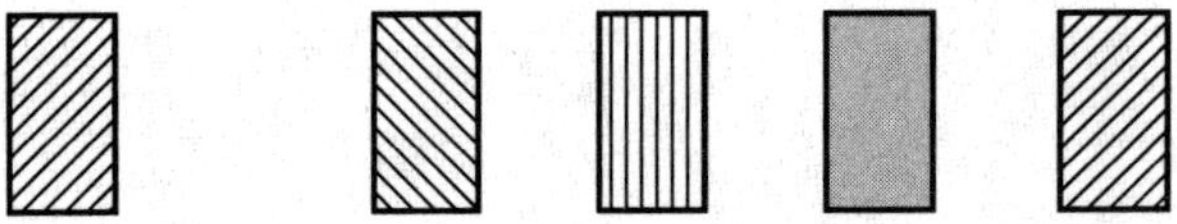

( )

29: 1 2 3 4

(   )

30: 1 2 3 4

(   )

31: 1 2 3 4

(   )

32: 1 2 3 4

(   )

Underline all consonants followed by a vowel and all vowels followed by a consonant.

33: N C J C I F T U Y E G D H J I T D R A A

34: B N M U I O W Q W Q A E Q C V T I P

35: Z X C V B N M E U I O U I D X E Q A X

36: A Z X L K J U I K J U R A R E R T Y U Z

Underline all even numbers followed by an odd number and all odd numbers followed by an even number.

37: 1 2 3 4 2 9 8 6 5 1 2 1 2 1 3 5 7 3 4 2 8 6 2 1

38: 1 7 9 7 5 7 4 3 5 7 9 5 3 2 4 8 0 6 4 3 5 7 8 5

39: 2 4 6 5 3 4 7 8 0 9 9 6 5 4 3 7 9 9 2 4 4 3 4 2

40: 6 9 6 5 5 7 8 6 6 7 6 5 4 7 9 7 6 4 0 2 2 9 0 2

Chapter 10

Tests for Children Aged 13–15

Verbal

Underline whether the following words have the SAME or a DIFFERENT meaning.

1:	FRAGILE **(SAME)**	UNBREAKABLE **(DIFFERENT)**
2:	BUFFOON **(SAME)**	JOKER **(DIFFERENT)**
3:	COMPREHENSIBLE **(SAME)**	COHERENT **(DIFFERENT)**
4:	ENTOURAGE **(SAME)**	ASSOCIATES **(DIFFERENT)**
5:	FLUCTUATING **(SAME)**	CONSTANT **(DIFFERENT)**
6:	SCRUPULOUS **(SAME)**	CORRUPT **(DIFFERENT)**

Fill in the missing letters so the words mean the same as the definition.

7: An outburst of bad temper.

T _ N _ R _ M

8: Specialized language concerned with a particular subject.

J _ R _ O _

9: To walk unsteadily as if about to fall.

S _ A _ G _ R

10: A platform where public speakers address an audience.

R _ S _ R _ M

11: Of the greatest importance.

P _ R _ M _ U _ T

12: Position of public attention.

L _ M _ L _ G _ T

Which two phrases are the closest in meaning?

13:

a. **Just in the nick of time.**
b. **Just the ticket.**
c. **Play the trump card.**
d. **Just what the doctor ordered.**

_ and _

14:

a. Seeing is believing.

b. Too many cooks spoil the broth.

c. The proof of the pudding is in the eating.

d. Out of sight, out of mind.

_ and _

15:

a. Hit the nail on the head.

b. A bad workman blames his tools.

c. To deal a hammer blow.

d. To be spot on.

_ and _

16:

a. Go by the book.

b. Follow the letter of the law.

c. Wasted talent is a crime.

d. Don't believe everything you read.

_ and _

Each item in column (c) belongs either to column (a) or to column (b). Underline which belongs to (a) and which belongs to (b).

17:

a	b	c		
APE	PUMA	LION	a	b
GORILLA	PANTHER	CHIMPANZEE	a	b
MONKEY	COUGAR	TIGER	a	b
		CHEETAH	a	b

18:

a	b	c		
CHAIR	CAR	BENCH	a	b
STOOL	BOAT	HELICOPTER	a	b
SETTEE	TRAIN	BICYCLE	a	b
		SOFA	a	b
		TRAM	a	b

19:

a	b	c		
CAP	SHOE	BOOT	a	b
BERET	CLOG	HAT	a	b
CROWN	SLIPPER	SANDAL	a	b
		TIARA	a	b
		SKATE	a	b

20:

a	b	c		
FUR	FINS	PAWS	a	b
WHISKERS	SCALES	GILLS	a	b
BASKET	BOWL	TANK	a	b
		CLAWS	a	b
		PURR	a	b

Underline the odd one out.

21:
a. PLAICE
b. CHICKEN
c. HADDOCK
d. COD

a b c d

22:
a. COBRA
b. STARLING
c. FINCH
d. MAGPIE

a b c d

23:
a. PAWN
b. DEACON
c. ROOK
d. QUEEN

a b c d

24:
a. BOOK
b. NEWSPAPER
c. TELEVISION
d. MAGAZINE

a b c d

25:
a. MANCHESTER
b. PLYMOUTH
c. NOTTINGHAM
d. PARIS

a b c d

Insert the word from the following anagrams.

26: **TOMA** ( )

27: **EOWRP** ( )

28: **ECLCRI** ( )

29: **NOTESHY** ( )

30: **NEARHOT** ( )

Underline whether the following jumbled sentences are TRUE or FALSE.

31: **SQUEAK EAT MOST CHEESE LIKE MICE TO AND**

(TRUE) (FALSE)

32: **A OCEAN CROSS SECONDS FEW CAN SWIMMER THE IN A**

(TRUE) (FALSE)

33: **THAT FOOTBALL GOALS IN TEAM MOST LOSES THE SCORES THE**

(TRUE) (FALSE)

34: **THE EAT PEOPLE IN BREAKFAST USUALLY MORNING**

(TRUE) (FALSE)

35: **DIFFERENT THERE ANIMALS THE LOTS ZOO ARE OF AT**

(TRUE) (FALSE)

36: **YOUR ARE TO SOCKS WARM KEEP SUPPOSED EARS**

(TRUE) (FALSE)

Make as many words as you can from the following words (3 letters or over).

37: VOWEL

a.	**d.**	**g.**
b.	**e.**	**h.**
c.	**f.**	**i.**

38: EXPECTED

a.	**i.**
b.	**j.**
c.	**k.**
d.	**l.**
e.	**m.**
f.	**n.**
g.	**o.**
h.	

39: COMBINE

1.	**11.**	**21.**
2.	**12.**	**22.**
3.	**13.**	**23.**
4.	**14.**	**24.**
5.	**15.**	**25.**
6.	**16.**	**26.**
7.	**17.**	**27.**
8.	**18.**	**28.**
9.	**19.**	**29.**
10.	**20.**	**30.**

40: DROUGHT

1.
2.
3.
4.
5.
6.
7.
8.
9.
10.
11.
12.
13.
14.
15.
16.
17.
18.
19.
20.
21.
22.
23.
24.
25.
26.
27.
28.
29.
30.
31.
32.
33.
34.
35.
36.
37.
38.
39.
40.
41.
42.
43.
44.
45.
46.
47.
48.
49.
50.

Chapter 11

Tests for Children Aged 13–15

Visuo-spatial

All blocks below are the same size and shape. Decide how many other blocks each block is touching and write this number in the table. Faces or sides touching count but corners do not.

1:

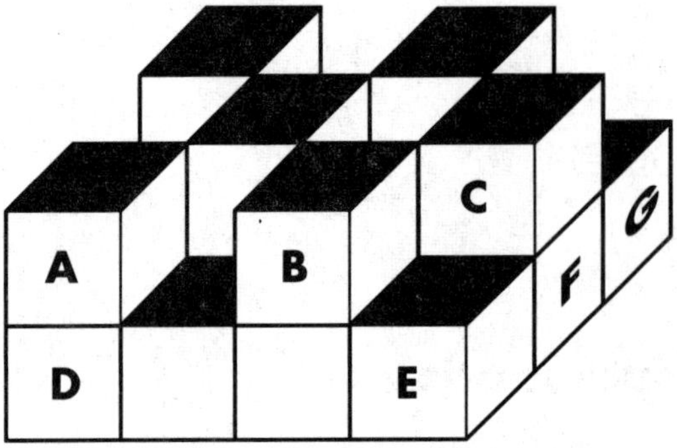

A	
B	
C	
D	
E	
F	
G	

2:

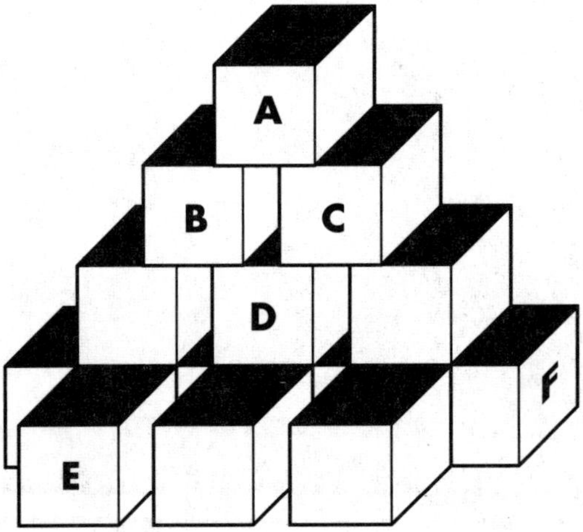

A	
B	
C	
D	
E	
F	

3:

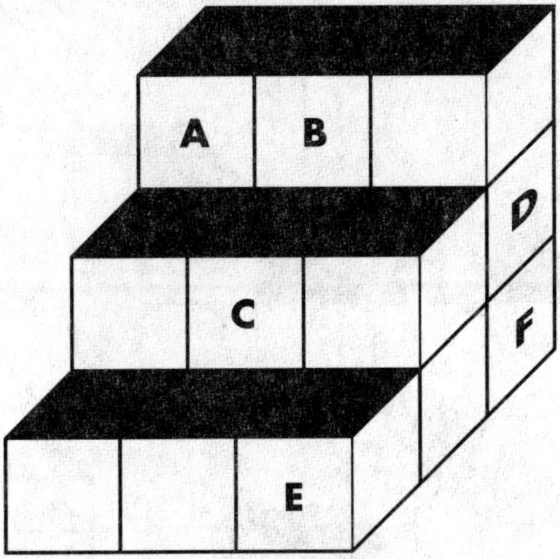

A	
B	
C	
D	
E	
F	

4:

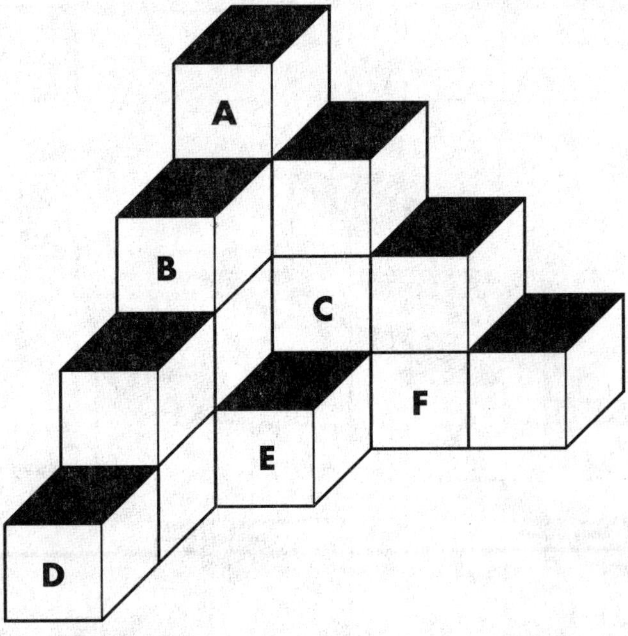

A	
B	
C	
D	
E	
F	

5:

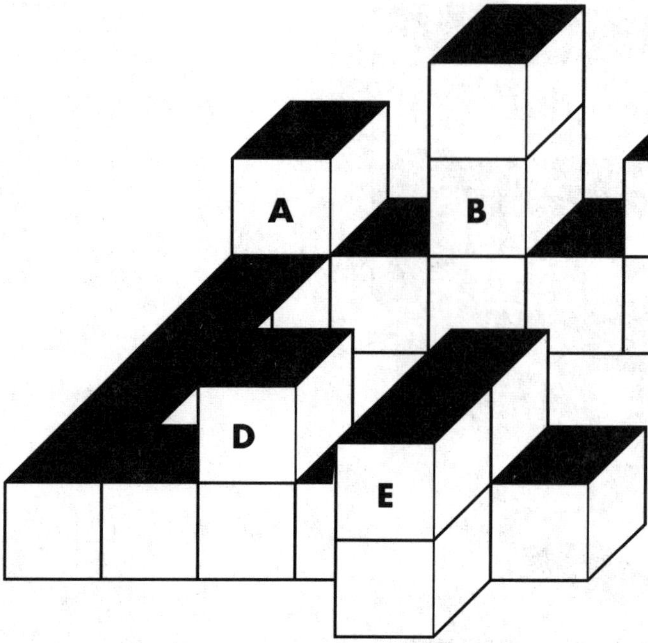

A	
B	
C	
D	
E	

6:

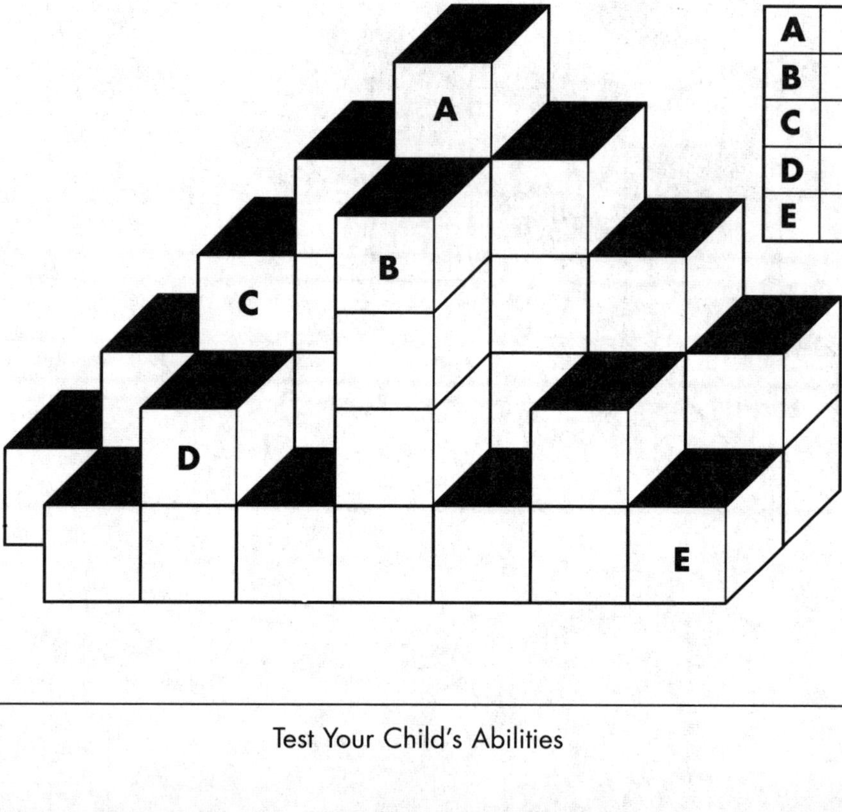

A	
B	
C	
D	
E	

Each side of the following cubes has a different design. If the cubes are rotated, underline whether they are the SAME or DIFFERENT.

7:

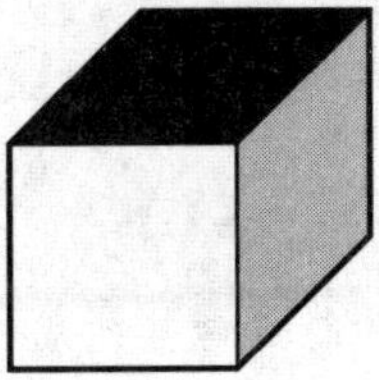

(SAME) **(DIFFERENT)**

8:

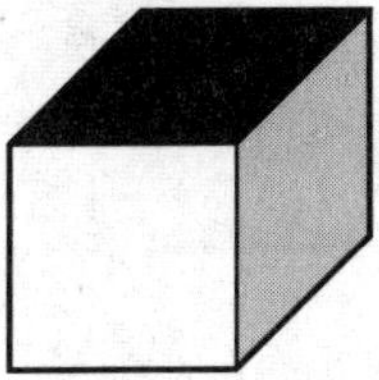

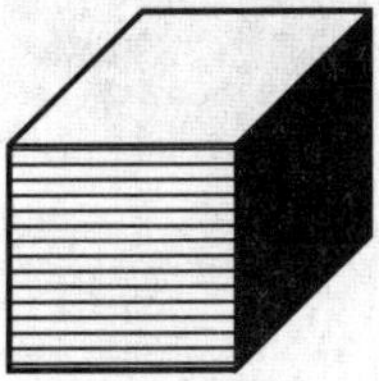

(SAME) **(DIFFERENT)**

9:

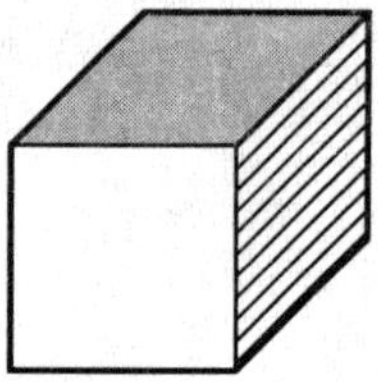

(SAME)

(DIFFERENT)

10:

(SAME)

(DIFFERENT)

11:

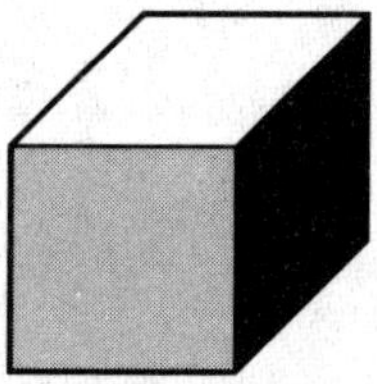

(SAME)

(DIFFERENT)

12:

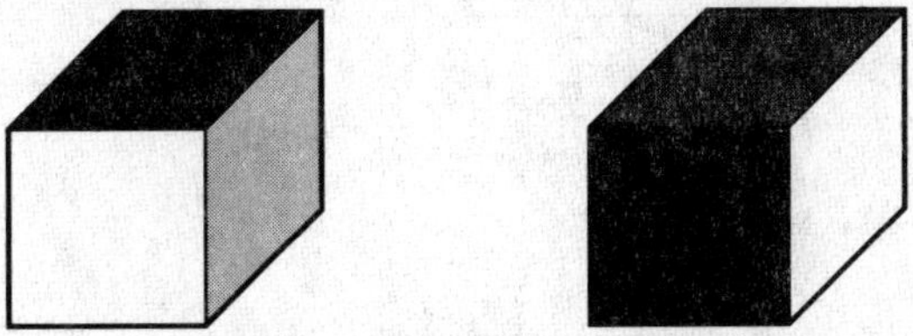

(SAME) **(DIFFERENT)**

Underline whether the two flags can be rotated into the same position.

13:

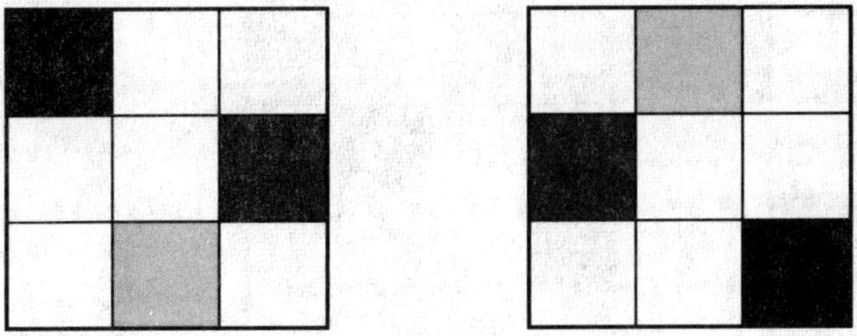

(YES) **(NO)**

14:

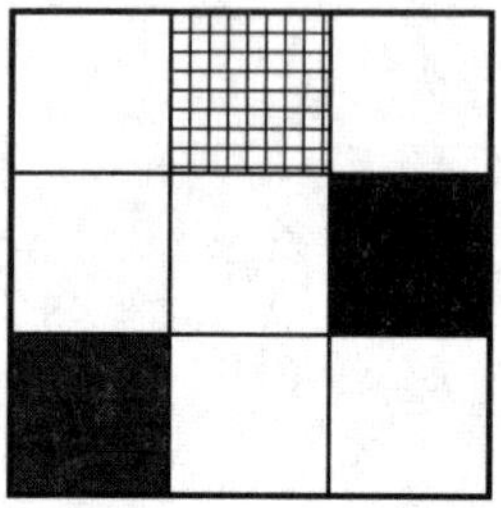

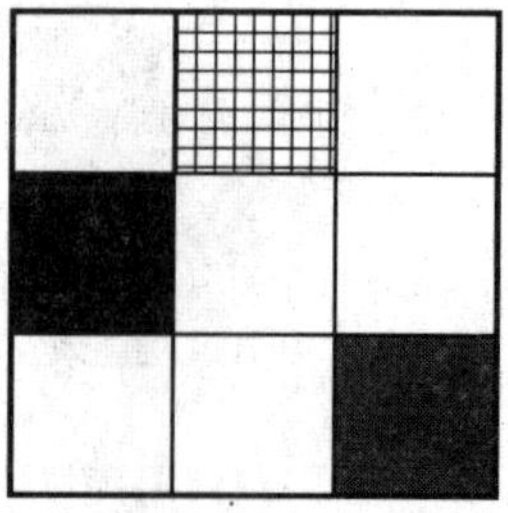

(YES) **(NO)**

15:

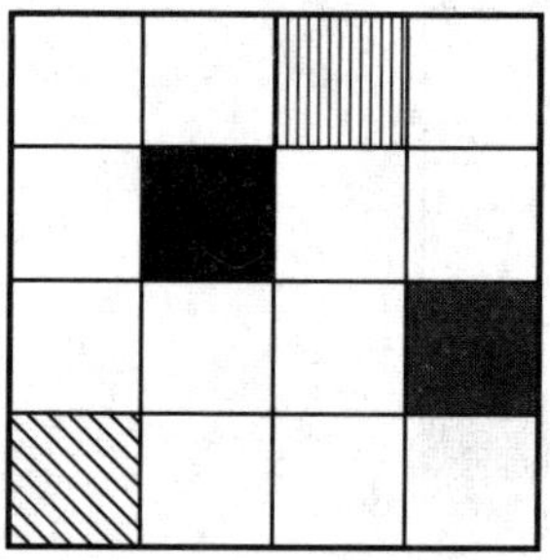

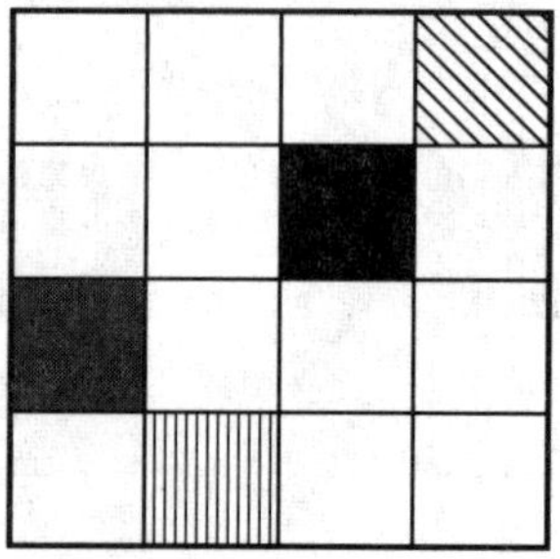

(YES) **(NO)**

16:  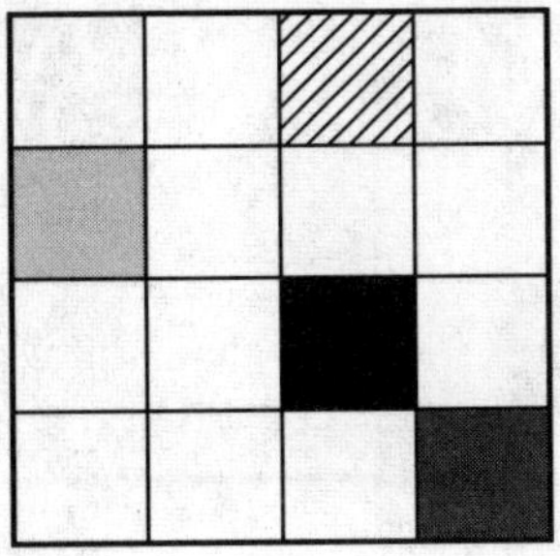

(YES) **(NO)**

17: 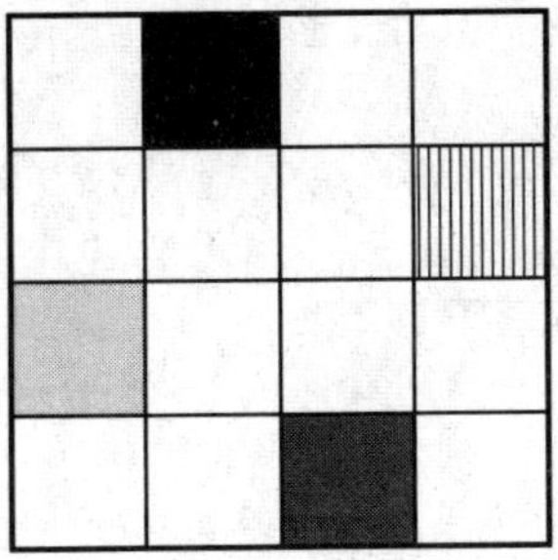 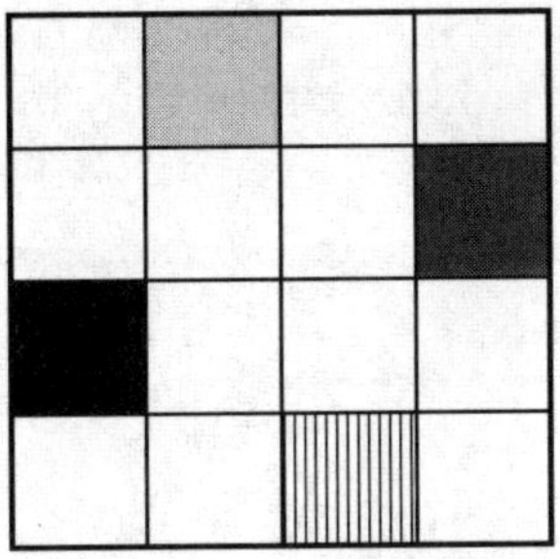

(YES) **(NO)**

18: 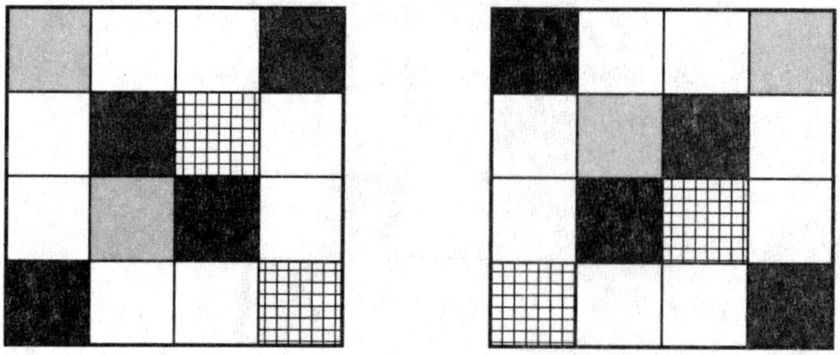

(YES) (NO)

The following shapes have been split into several pieces. Draw the pieces in the whole shape to show how they fit.

19: 

20: 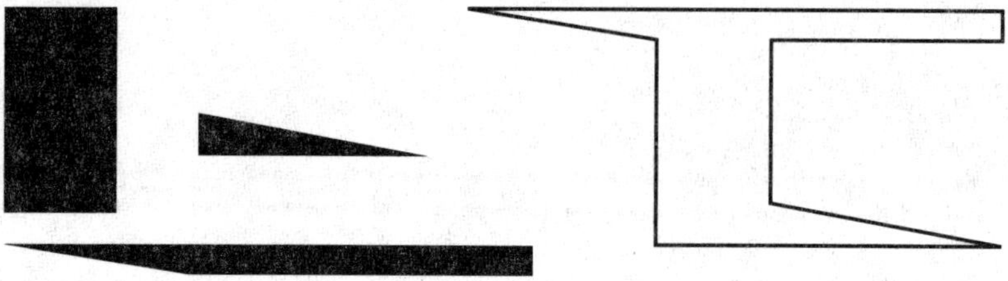

21:

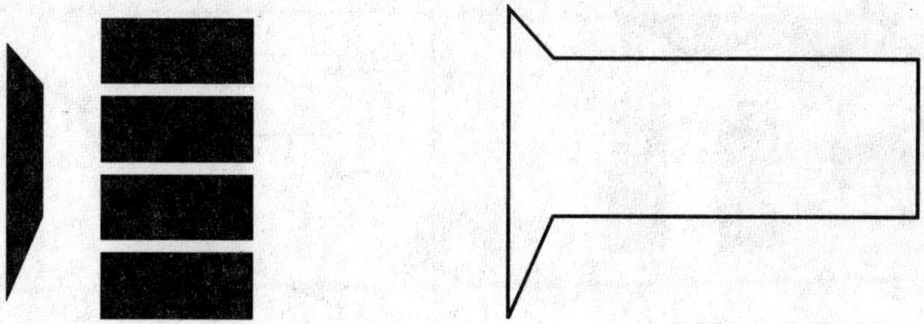

22:

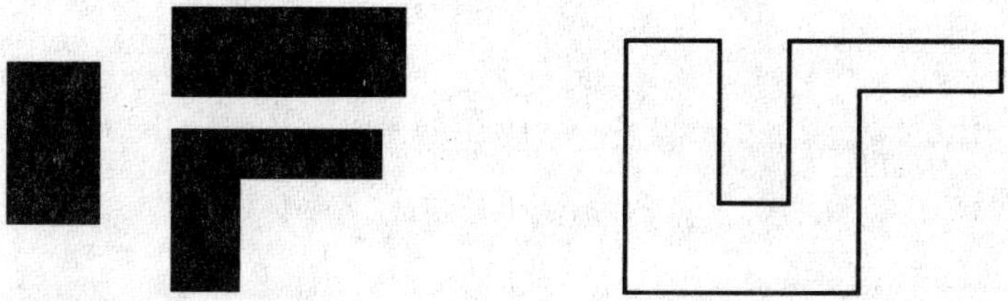

23:

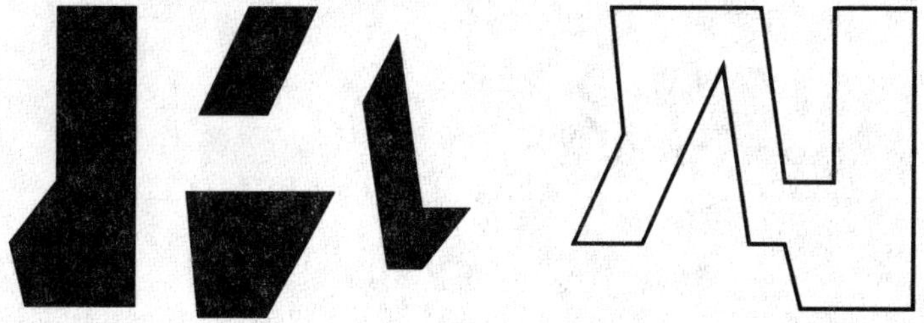

24:

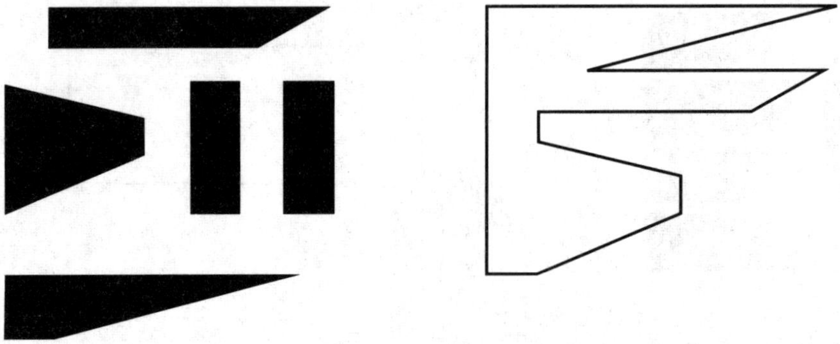

Underline whether the two diagrams show the SAME side of the card or the OPPOSITE side.

25:

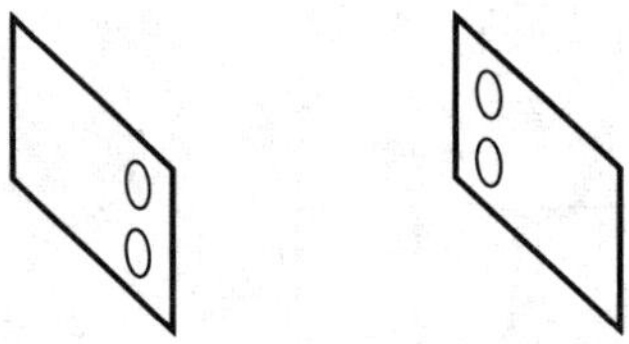

(SAME) **(OPPOSITE)**

26:

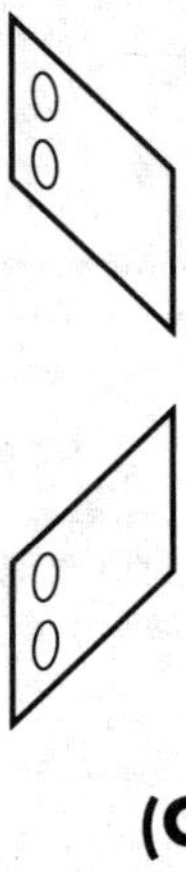

(SAME) **(OPPOSITE)**

27:

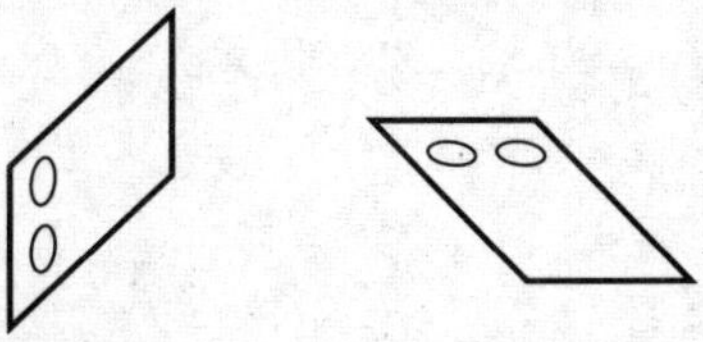

(SAME) **(OPPOSITE)**

28:

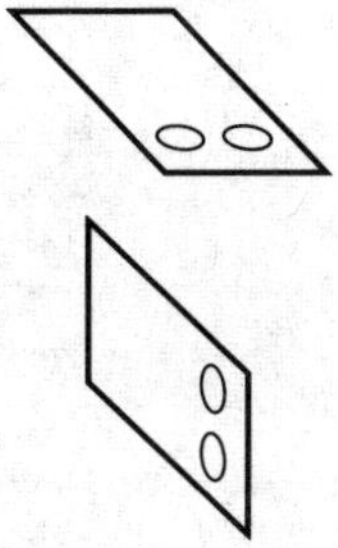

(SAME) **(OPPOSITE)**

29:

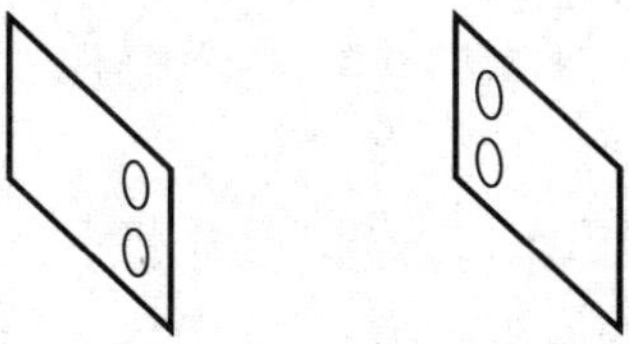

(SAME) **(OPPOSITE)**

30:

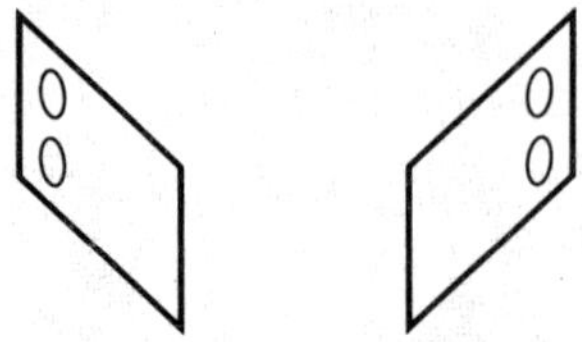

(SAME) (OPPOSITE)

Underline the symbol which is the odd one out.

31: A B C D E

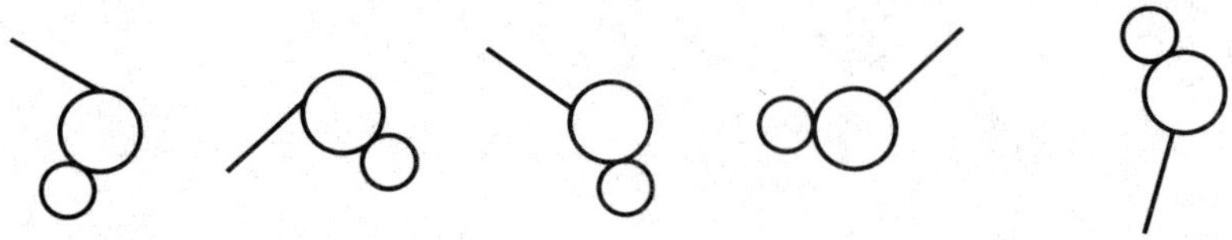

32: A B C D E

33: A B C D E

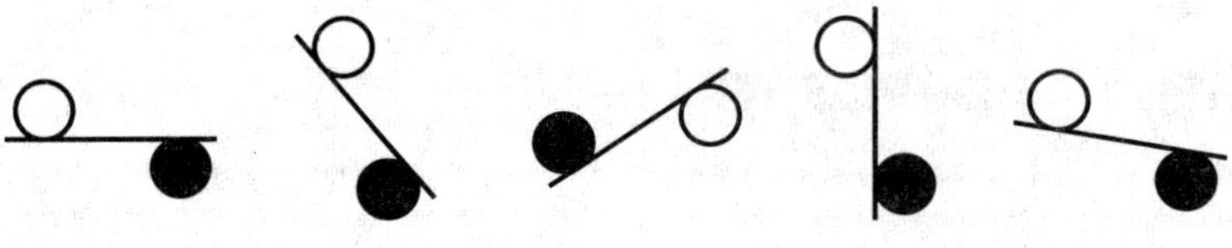

34: A B C D E

35:

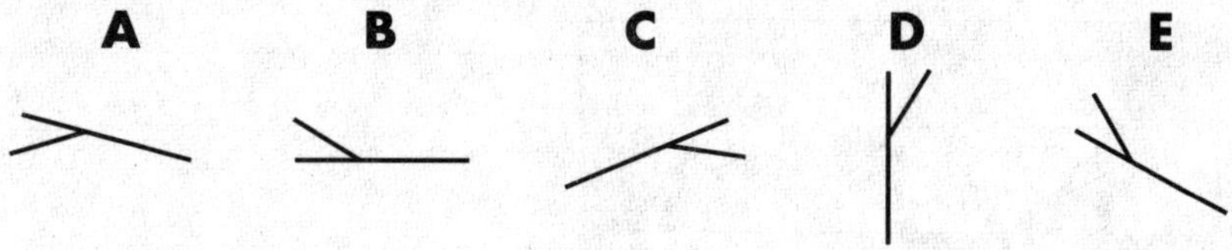

How many black squares are there? Write this number in the box.

36:

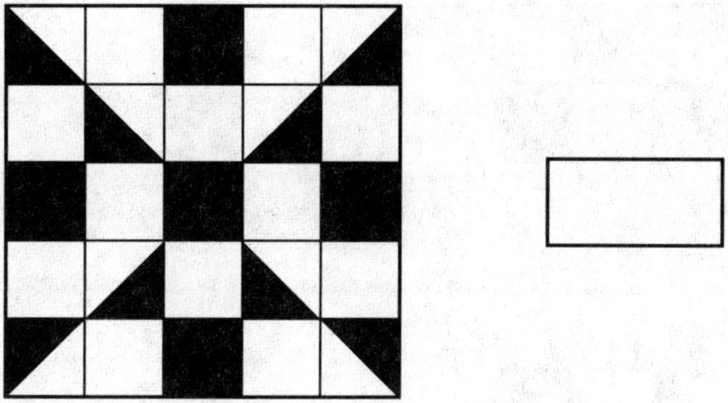

37:

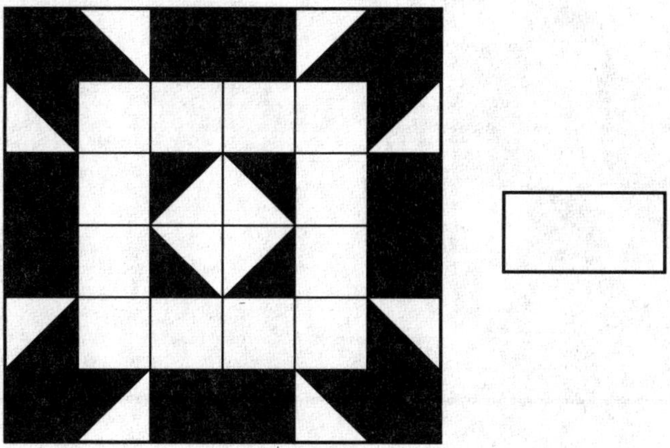

38:

39:

40:

Chapter 12

Test Scoring System for Children Aged 13–15

Chapter 7

Questions 1–40:	2 points for each totally correct answer

Chapter 8

Questions 1–5:	1 point for each totally correct answer
Questions 6–25:	2 points for each totally correct answer
Questions 26–35:	per question: 3 parts correct = 1 point, 6 = 2, 7 = 3 and 11 = 4
Questions 36–40:	per question: 2 parts correct = 1 point, 5 = 2, 8 = 3

Chapter 9

Questions 1–5:	1 point for each totally correct answer
Questions 6–32:	2 points for each totally correct answer
Questions 33–40:	per question: 6 parts correct = 1 point, 9 = 2 and 11 = 4

Chapter 10

Questions 1–36:	1 point for each totally correct answer
Question 37:	3 words correct = 1 point, 6 = 2, 7 = 4 and 8 = 6
Question 38:	5 words correct = 1 point, 10 = 2, 13 = 4 and 14 = 6
Question 39:	6 words correct = 1 point, 12 = 2, 18 = 4, 24 = 8, 25 = 9 and 26 = 10
Question 40:	5 words correct = 1 point, 10 = 2, 15 = 4, 20 = 6, 25 = 8, 30 = 10, 35 = 12, 40 = 14, 45 = 16, 46 = 19 and 47 = 22

Chapter 11

Question 1:	3 parts correct = 1 point, 7 = 2
Questions 2–4:	3 parts correct = 1 point, 6 = 2
Questions 5–6:	3 parts correct = 1 point, 5 = 2
Questions 7–40:	2 points for each totally correct answer

Abstract Reasoning

1: **69**

2: **80**

3: **243**

4: **67**

5: **41**

6: **79**

7: **W**

8: **G**

9: **I**

10: **V**

11: **J**

12: **E, G**

13: **True**

14: **False**

15: **False**

16: **False**

17: **False**

18: **False**

19: **False**

20: **True**

21: **False**

22: **True**

23: **True**

24: **4**

25: **2**

26: **3**

27: **1**

28: **5**

29: **2**

30: **2**

31: **1**

32: **3**

33: **1**

34: **4**

35: **4**

36: **2**

37: **1**

38: **2**

39: **1**

40: **4**

Numerical

1: **(4 + 8) – (2 + 5) = 5**

2: **(3 x 7) + (9 – 6) = 24**

3: **(4 + 6) / (7 – 5) = 5**

4: **(5 + 9) x (6 / 2) = 42**

5: **(5 x 8) / (2 x 4) = 5**

6: **144**

7: **£4.47**

8: **7**

9: **1682 seconds or 28 minutes and 2 seconds**

10: **5**

11: **3**

12: **5 or 11**

13: **4**

14: **14**

15: **30**

16: **60**

17: **512**

18: **18**

19: **18**

20: **7**

21: **17**

22: **72**

23: **5**

24: **5**

25: **27 or –22**

26:

Cinema Audiences

	Morning	Afternoon	Evening	Total
Adult	48	86	50	184
Child	52	148	100	300
Total	100	234	150	484

27:

Ice-Cream Sales

	Cone	Tub	Scoop	Lolly	Total
Small	58	10	39	25	132
Medium	86	25	62	48	221
Large	22	50	2	26	100
Total	166	85	103	99	453

28:

Music Sales

	Jazz	Soul	Dance	Other	Total
Male	38	32	54	42	166
Female	46	34	32	38	150
Group	18	27	49	26	120
Total	102	93	135	106	436

29:

Tournament Entries

	U–10	U–14	U–18	Open	Total
Male	45	56	67	78	246
Female	18	36	54	22	130
Doubles	24	48	36	16	124
Total	87	140	157	116	500

30:

Buffet Sales

	Tea	Coffee	Crisps	Nuts	Total
Small	103	89	59	36	287
Medium	67	58	28	11	164
Large	43	123	46	95	307
Total	213	270	133	142	758

31:

10	13	19	9	6
27	5	11	12	2
16	3	18	13	7
6	27	1	18	5

32:

12	23	34	45
34	45	12	23
45	34	23	12
23	12	45	34

33:

36	17	28	42
28	42	36	17
42	28	17	36
17	36	42	28

34:

23	25	14	16	12
14	12	25	23	16
12	23	16	14	25
16	14	12	25	23
25	16	23	12	14

35:

16	38	41	34	49
41	49	38	16	34
49	16	34	41	38
34	41	49	38	16
38	34	16	49	41

36:
a. 3 + 9
b. 4 + 8
c. 5 + 7

37:
a. 4 + 6 + 9
b. 3 + 7 + 9
c. 2 + 8 + 9
d. 8 + 7 + 4
e. 8 + 6 + 5

38:
a. 2 x 3 x 5
b. 1 x 5 x 6

39:
a. 9 + 5 + 1
b. 9 + 4 + 2
c 8 + 6 + 1
d. 8 + 5 + 2
e. 8 + 4 + 3
f. 7 + 6 + 2
g. 7 + 5 + 3
h. 6 + 5 + 4

40:
a. 1 x 5 x 8
b. 2 x 4 x 5

Perceptual

1: **d**

2: **b**

3: **a**

4: **d**

5: **c**

6:

code	translation
+) # & $	CRAFT
& = > # $	FLOAT
+) £ £ @	CREEP
@ [£ + £	PIECE

7:

code	translation
& £ (> + £	BEFORE
$ = + + > <	CARROT
# £ ! £ @ #	DEPEND
= + > %@ #	AROUND
& + £ £ * £	BREEZE

8:

code	translation
< & (£ $ >	REMIND
% # $ # @ <	HONOUR
< ! > £) %	RADISH
* £ $ £) %	FINISH
(& $! + &	MENACE

9:

code	translation
* # $ ((£ >	SHATTER
> £ (& > £ *	RETIRES
(@ > > £ < (	TORRENT
* + & ((£ <	SMITTEN
* (> & = £ *	STRIPES
= £ > ~ £ [(	PERFECT

10:

code	translation
+ (* % > < *	TREMBLE
@ (! $ $ < *	WRIGGLE
* & + ( ) £ +	EXTRACT
) ~ ~ * > (=	APPEARS
* (( ) + ! £	ERRATIC
£ # % ~ < * [	COMPLEX

11: **Different**

12: **Same**

13: **Different**

14: **Same**

15: **Same**

16: **Different**

17: **Different**

18: **Different**

19: **Same**

20: **Different**

21: **Same**

22: **Different**

23: **QTN or 306**

24: **SQOT or 1350**

25: **LPKQ or 8493**

26: **R or 2**

27: **NNMT or 6670**

28: **4**

29: **3**

30: **1**

31: **3**

32: **3**

33: N C J **C** **I** F **T** **U** **Y** **E** G D H **J** **I** T D **R** A A

34: B N **M** U I **O** W Q W **Q** A **E** Q C V **T** **I** P

35: Z X C V B N **M** E U I O U **I** D **X** **E** **Q** **A** X

36: **A** Z X L K **J** U **I** K **J** **U** **R** **A** **R** **E** R T **Y** **U** Z

37: **1** **2** **3** 4 **2** **9** 8 **6** 5 **1** **2** **1** **2** 1 3 5 7 **3** 4 2 8 6 **2** 1

38: 1 7 9 7 5 **7** **4** 3 5 7 9 5 **3** 2 4 8 0 6 **4** 3 5 **7** **8** 5

39: 2 4 **6** 5 **3** **4** **7** 8 **0** 9 **9** **6** **5** **4** 3 7 9 **9** 2 4 **4** **3** 4 2

40: **6** **9** **6** 5 5 **7** 8 6 **6** **7** **6** **5** **4** 7 9 **7** 6 4 0 2 **2** **9** 0 2

Verbal

1: **Different**

2: **Same**

3: **Same**

4: **Same**

5: **Different**

6: **Different**

7: **Tantrum**

8: **Jargon**

9: **Stagger**

10: **Rostrum**

11: **Paramount**

12: **Limelight**

13: **b and d**

14: **a and c**

15: **a and d**

16: **a and b**

17:	**Lion**	**b**
	Chimpanzee	**a**
	Tiger	**b**
	Cheetah	**b**
18:	**Bench**	**a**
	Helicopter	**b**
	Bicycle	**b**
	Sofa	**a**
	Tram	**b**
19:	**Boot**	**b**
	Hat	**a**
	Sandal	**b**
	Tiara	**a**
	Skate	**b**
20:	**Paws**	**a**
	Gills	**b**
	Tank	**b**
	Claws	**a**
	Purr	**a**

21: **b**

22: **a**

23: **b**

24: **c**

25: **d**

26: **Atom or Moat**

27: **Power**

28: **Circle or Cleric**

29: **Honesty**

30: **Another**

31: **True**

32: **False**

33: **False**

34: **True**

35: **True**

36: **False**

37:	VOW	VOLE	OWE	OWL	LEV	
	WOVE	WOE	LOVE	LOW		
38:	EXPECT	EXCEPT	EXCEPTED	PEED		
	EXCEED	EPEE	PET	TED		
	CEDE	TEPEE	TEE	CEP		
	TEED	DEEP	PEE			
39:	COMB	COME	COB	COIN	CON	NOME
	CONE	OMEN	ONCE	ONE	MOB	BONCE
	MICE	MINCE	MINE	MIEN	MEN	BEN
	BONE	BIN	ICON	ICE	ION	COMBE
	INCOME	NOB	NICE	NIB	BINE	BICE
40:	DRUG	DOUR	DOUGH	DOG	TOG	
	DOH	DOT	DUO	DUG	UGH	
	ROD	ROUGH	ROUT	ROT	TOD	
	RUG	RUT	RHO	OUR	TROG	
	OUGHT	OUT	GROUT	GOD	GROT	
	GOURD	GOUT	GOT	GUT	DOTH	
	HOD	HOUR	HOG	HOT	TRUG	
	HURT	HUG	HUT	TROD	RUTH	
	TROUGH	TOR	TOUR	TOUGH	DROUTH	
	TUG	THOU	THUD	THUG	DOR	

Visuo-spatial

1:	A: 4	E: 5
	B: 6	F: 6
	C: 6	G: 5
	D: 4	
2:	A: 2	D: 5
	B: 3	E: 3
	C: 3	F: 2
3:	A: 4	D: 8
	B: 6	E: 4
	C: 8	F: 6
4:		
	A: 3	D: 2
	B: 6	E: 6
	C: 9	F: 5
5:	A: 3	D: 3
	B: 4	E: 3
	C: 2	
6:	A: 4	D: 8
	B: 6	E: 5
	C: 6	

7: **Same**

8: **Different**

9: **Same**

10: **Same**

11: **Different**

12: **Different**

13: **Yes**

14: **No**

15: **No**

16: **Yes**

17: **No**

18: **Yes**

19: 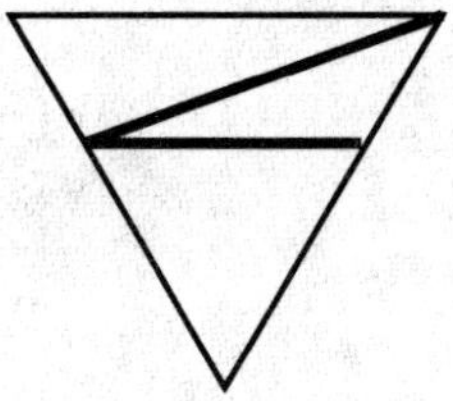

20: 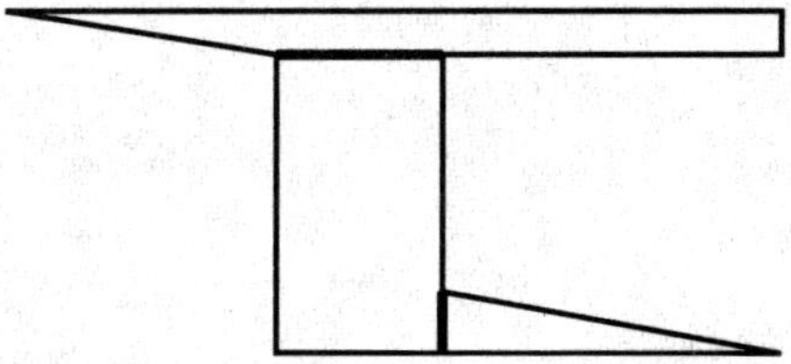

21: 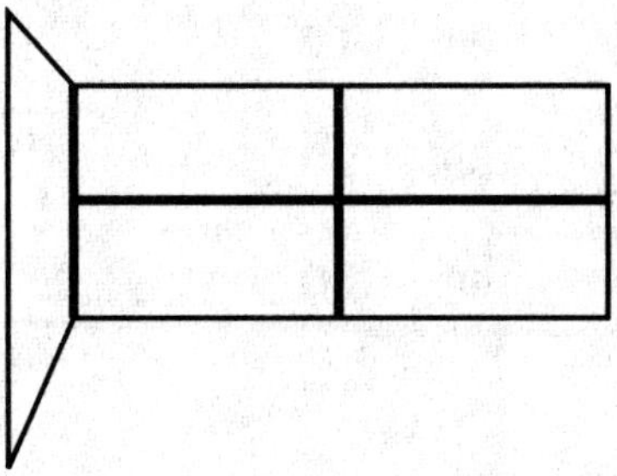

22:

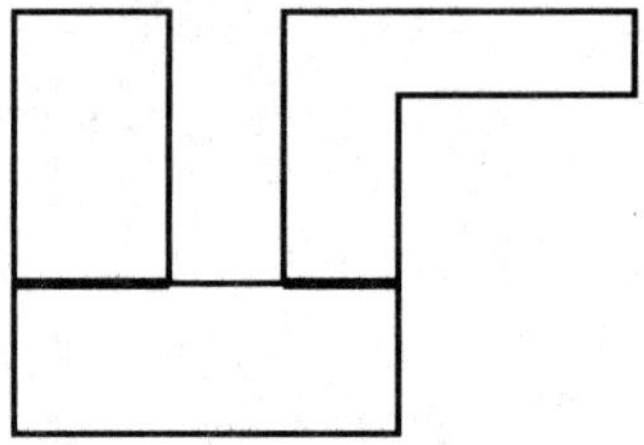

23:

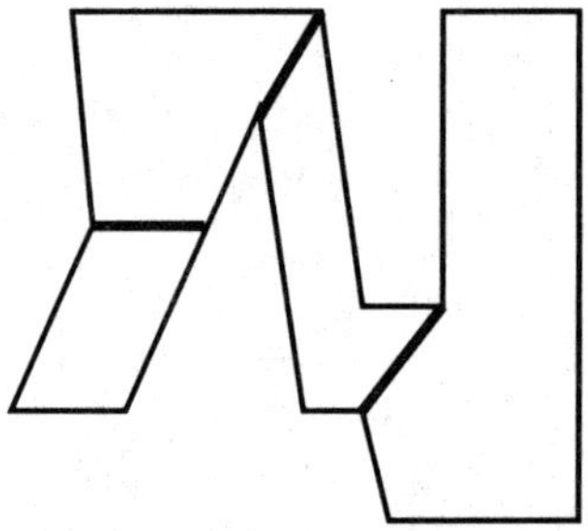

24:

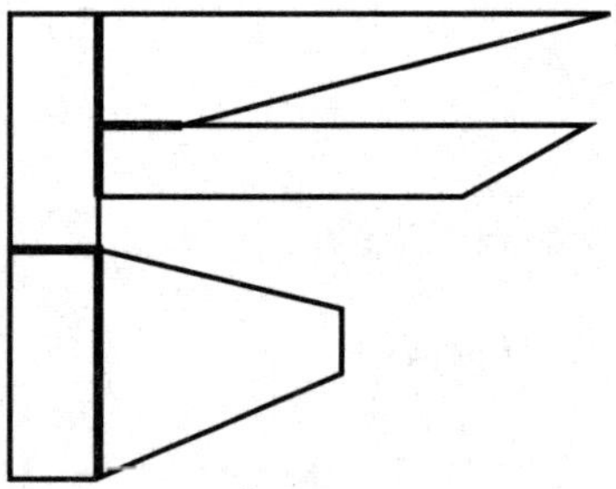

25: **Same**

26: **Opposite**

27: **Same**

28: **Opposite**

29: **Same**

30: **Opposite**

31: **E**

32: **D**

33: **D**

34: **D**

35: **A**

36: **9**

37: **18**

38: **12**

39: **20**

40: **20**

Profile of Abilities and IQ Conversion Tables

IQ and Profile of Abilities for Children Aged 13–15

The first step is to score each of the five ability tests. Having done that, look at the Test Score Table appropriate for your age, and see whether your score on each of the five tests is in the Outstanding, Excellent, Very Good, Good, Adequate or Fair category. Now look at the table below and put an X in the category you have achieved. The pattern of X marks is a profile of your abilities.

	Test 7 **Abstract Reasoning**	**Test 8** **Numerical**	**Test 9** **Perceptual**	**Test 10** **Verbal**	**Test 11** **Visuo-spatial**
1 Outstanding					
2 Excellent					
3 Very Good					
4 Good					
5 Adequate					
6 Fair					

Test Score Table for Children Aged 13

	Test 7 Abstract Reasoning	Test 8 Numerical	Test 9 Perceptual	Test 10 Verbal	Test 11 Visuo-spatial
1 Oustanding	Above 71	Above 51	Above 71	Above 43	Above 67
2 Excellent	62–71	42–51	65–71	37–43	58–67
3 Very Good	52–61	32–41	58–64	30–36	48–57
4 Good	42–51	22–31	51–57	23–29	38–47
5 Adequate	32–41	12–21	44–50	16–22	28–37
6 Fair	Below 32	Below 12	Below 44	Below 16	Below 28

Test Score Table for Children Aged 14

	Test 7 **Abstract Reasoning**	**Test 8** **Numerical**	**Test 9** **Perceptual**	**Test 10** **Verbal**	**Test 11** **Visuo-spatial**
1 Outstanding	Above 73	Above 53	Above 73	Above 46	Above 71
2 Excellent	64–73	44–53	67–73	40–46	62–71
3 Very Good	54–63	34–43	60–66	33–39	52–61
4 Good	44–53	24–33	53–59	26–32	42–51
5 Adequate	34–43	14–23	46–52	19–25	32–41
6 Fair	Below 34	Below 14	Below 46	Below 19	Below 32

Test Score Table for Children Aged 15

	Test 7 Abstract Reasoning	Test 8 Numerical	Test 9 Perceptual	Test 10 Verbal	Test 11 Visuo-spatial
1 Outstanding	Above 75	Above 55	Above 75	Above 49	Above 75
2 Excellent	66–75	46–55	69–75	43–49	66–75
3 Very Good	56–65	36–45	62–68	36–42	56–65
4 Good	46–55	26–35	55–61	29–35	46–55
5 Adequate	36–45	16–25	48–54	22–28	36–45
6 Fair	Below 36	Below 16	Below 48	Below 22	Below 36

IQ Conversion Table for Children
Aged 13–15 Years

To obtain your IQ, add together all five of your ability scores. Enter this total score at the bottom of the IQ Conversion Table below. Find the appropriate age level and read off the IQ corresponding to your score.

Score			Intelligence
Age 13	Age 14	Age 15	IQ
350	370	390	150
330	350	370	145
310	330	350	140
290	310	330	135
270	290	310	130
250	270	290	125
230	250	270	120
210	230	250	115
190	210	230	110
170	190	210	105
150	170	190	100
	Score:	IQ:	